THE WELL BY THE WAY

THE WELL
BY THE WAY

A SECOND BOOK OF COUNSEL AND COMPANY FOR THE SABBATH EVENING

By ALEXANDER SMELLIE, D.D.

> " As they traverse the valley of tears
>   They make it a place of fountains,
>   Clothed with the blessings of early rain :
> From rampart to rampart on they march,
>   Till at last God revealeth Himself in Zion."
>
> PSALM lxxxiv.,
> in Professor J. E. McFADYEN'S Translation

SECOND EDITION

LONDON: ANDREW MELROSE LTD.
3 YORK STREET, COVENT GARDEN, W.C. 2

First Published . . . *December 1918*
Reprinted . . . . . *September 1920*

CONTENTS

THE WELL BY THE WAY

I

WITHOUT THE WAY THERE IS NO GOING

WE resemble the first disciples of Our Lord. Our destination is concealed in the meantime. If the ultimate future is far from being dark, it is so partially disclosed that we can draw no detailed map of it. Over its "fair dells and groves," as Henry Vaughan designates them, a mist hangs, like that other mist which kept the heart of Eden green. But, although the goal is largely hidden, the road to it is bathed in sun. The consummation may lie in a golden haze that dazzles us with excess of light; but the path is accessible and clear. What Christ said to the disciples He says to us,

THE WELL BY THE WAY

Whither I go ye know the Way (John xiv. 4). For the Way is Himself.

I

We know the Way. It is the road of the Loving Heart.

" Considering the love of his Excellency Tusitala in his care for us in our tribulation, we have made this gift; it shall never be muddy, it shall go on for ever, the road that we have dug "—this was the beautiful inscription which the Samoans put up over the new approach they made through the brushwood to Stevenson's house in Vailima. Some of them had been in prison for a political offence, and he showed them whatever kindness he could; now, openly and practically, they gave him their thanks. No wonder was it that he was deeply touched. " The Road of Loving Hearts " he called the path which they had toiled willingly to construct. But that was love going out in response to sympathy and graciousness manifested and experienced. Christ's road was altogether different. It was made before any sympathy or graciousness was

2

visible, and made to bring Him near to us who were filled with suspicions and dislikes and positive enmities. It led Him from a far distance into closest proximity and union with you and me. Till, through condescension and self-emptying and goodness and mercy, He has overcome our inveterate antagonism. Till He has won our faith. Till He has captured our affection. Till His love unknown has broken every barrier down. And now He is, for each of us, the Way. Not only are we to receive Him; we are to follow Him, too, in the strength of His Holy Spirit. First we yield ourselves to Him, and to God revealed in Him; and then we yield ourselves to our fellow-men. No lethargy or selfishness on our side, and no incompatibilities on theirs, are to prevent us from succouring, cheering, blessing them. This is the Road of Loving Hearts, and it goes on for ever, on until it arrives "at Heaven's gate built in Jerusalem's wall." It convoys us to where Christ is, and where many friends of His and ours are with Him —the city "whose citizens are lovely and whose King is Very Love."

II

We know the Way. It is the road of the Righteous Soul.

Somewhere in the *Pensées*, Pascal says that he is the noblest man in whom attributes which seem contradictory blend without a jar. But in no one were such complementary features reconciled so absolutely as in Jesus Christ. If love governed Him morning and night, righteousness was the passion of His heart in living and in dying. He never swerved from the straight line of God's commandment, and God's inexorable judgment on sin won His deep and ready Amen. *Jesus Christ the Righteous*, that apostle named Him who understood Him best; and the crystalline diadem does befit His brow. This, also, is our road—the road of the righteous soul. Guilty, lost, and helpless, we take His righteousness to justify us in God's sight. We are done for ever with the filthy garments that, through many a year, had a strange fascination for us. We stand complete in the glorious and beautiful vesture of our great High Priest, and His fair mitre is on our sinful heads. But then we are enamoured of the untainted and stately righteousness ourselves. The law of the Lord is the tune to which we key our history each morning, to which we march during the day, and which is still singing through us at nightfall. It is a strong and searching tune. There is no easy sentiment in it. There is no " Dorian mood of flutes and soft recorders." It teaches us to condemn every departure from the good and acceptable and perfect Will. It renders us conscientious in the particularities and minutenesses of character and conduct. And how we reverence those whose lives, like Christ's, are set to the impressive music of righteousness ! She glowed with " one superb quality in which I only glimmer," Christina Rossetti wrote of her mother, Frances Polidori—the quality of " Justice." To be, by God's transforming Spirit, unchangingly just is to be on the road to where Jesus is. Having put on His " broidered coat," woven without seam throughout, we respond habitually to its appeal, and are resolved to walk everywhere in harmony with its radiance.

5

III

And we know the Way. It is the road of the Humble Spirit.

Jesus, knowing that the Father had given all things into His hands, and that He came out from God and went unto God, rose from supper, and fastened round His waist the apron of a slave, and stooped to wash the dusty feet of the men who were too angry and too proud to fulfil the lowly office for one another. To Him there was no incongruity in an origin so sublime, and a destiny so unparalleled, being linked with a bondservant's menial work. He was on earth just that He might do such self-negating things. He was priestly, princely, divine, when He performed the tasks some of us despise. But we may not despise them any longer, if we are His. The way, for us as for Him, is the way of the humble spirit. In one sense, we have nothing of which to boast. We were lifted from the horrible pit by His grace, and we are sustained in the holy life by His power ; we write George Herbert's motto over ourselves, " Less than the least of all His mercies." In another sense, we

6

are invested with august and incalculable dignity. We, too, have come forth from God, and are going to God. From the King's palace we descended, and to the King's palace we return. Yet we are always to count it a singular gladness and an enriching honour, when we are permitted to gird on the slave's towel and serve. The saints of whom we are most certain that they are with Christ in the better country are the saints who, when they were here, forgot themselves and preferred others. On the tombstone of one of them are written the Greek words, Ἐν πραυτῆτι σοφίας, *In meekness of wisdom*; for, though he was wise to enlighten everybody who listened to him, he was too humble to suspect his own greatness. Of the death-bed of another it is narrated : " Then, after a short pause, he suddenly said, ' You go first, I follow.' These eminently characteristic words were the last he spoke, and as his brother knelt and prayed the end came." God make you and me like them ! God keep us constantly in the Valley where our Lord in former days had His country-house !

IV

We know the Way. It is the road of the Sacrificial Life—the life laid down to be taken again, and lost to be found.

Christ went straight from the Upper Room to bitter death. For the joy that lay before Him He patiently endured the Cross, and looked with contempt upon the shame. His sacrifice has its incommunicable character. It is vicarious, atoning, redemptive. It is our salvation, and the salvation of ten thousand times ten thousand. There we cannot reproduce Him. There He is without partner or comrade or helper. We can only praise Him for the life He purchased for our unworthy souls by the shedding of His blood. Yet, none the less, He summons us to sacrifice. *The Lord, He it is that doth go before thee*, even along this dread and blessed path. In all souls which truly belong to Him the soldierly principle of self-denial is uppermost and innermost. The Ego, the I, the temper which exalts ourselves, is dethroned. It has received its mortal wound. Now it is the Lord Who is enthroned.

Pierce deep and deeper, till you have laid bare our heart; and you will find—the Emperor. And over our life, from its centre to its circumference, He is Despot; for we are not staggered now by that stupendous New Testament name, with all its implications and all its consequences. Our daily prayer is that we may lose ourselves, obliterate ourselves, crucify ourselves, for His cause, for His people, and for Himself. Our daily confession is, *I must decrease, He must increase.* So we lay down our own lives; and we are in the Way which Christ went, and which is Christ; and soon we shall behold His face in righteousness, and be satisfied when we awake with His likeness.

II

GOD'S EVANGELIST OF THE SKY

PROBABLY there were rainbows before the Flood. Science informs us that in certain conditions of the atmosphere they are sure to be born; and it seems as if they must have repeated themselves, ever since sun and shower commenced to be. But, when the great catastrophe was over and finished, the rainbow gained a new distinction and was lifted into a new glory. For the first time it became a sacrament, and God ordained it to be His prophet. *I do set My bow in the cloud,* He said (Genesis ix. 13).

Nothing helps us more than to listen to this evangelist of His.

I

It will preach the friendliness of His thought.

Curious it is that, in Old Testament and

New, the Hebrew and Greek words for the bow in the sky are the very words belonging by right to the bow of battle and war, that wings its fatal arrows, and turns not back from the blood of the slain. It is almost as if God were emphasizing His desire to discard the one for the other, the weapon of His anger for the emblem and pronouncement of His peace. Or, if you should judge this far-fetched, we may look at it more simply. Nothing is heavenlier than the rainbow, yet nothing is so eager to touch and kiss the earth. It refuses to dwell, high and inaccessible, up in that blue vault above our heads. It is a bridge, whose keystone may be far off, but whose piers plant themselves on the homely ground. Even so, God, Who is Inhabitant of eternity, comes out and down to meet us, and His thought is the thought of a Friend. Genesis proves it. If the Flood is the dread verdict of incorruptible Holiness on scornful and incurable sin, the rainbow follows the Flood, and the rainbow is the King's envoy with the flag of reconciliation. "I was angry with thee," it says, "but Mine anger is turned away, and now I comfort thee."

But it is Christ Who dispels all the doubts. He is God's heaven stooping to the earth, embracing the earth, dignifying and redeeming the sinful and self-destroyed earth. Seneca, who was near the Kingdom—" our Seneca," Jerome called him with the *desiderium* of yearning and affection—confessed the weakness of his Stoicism, and pleaded with a pathetic cry, " None of us has strength to rise, and O that some one would stretch out a hand ! " Some One has stretched out a Hand, declining to remain apart from us, assuming our nature that He might exhaust our curse and free us from our death. And that Some One is God Himself in Jesus Christ. The bow in the sky loves and etherealizes a world which has wandered far and fallen very low.

II

No less convincingly the evangelist publishes the wideness of God's mercy.

What a scope and magnificence of sweep the bow in the cloud has ! When we see it in its entirety, it spans our horizon ; and no bridge of man's construction equals the bridge built in an instant out of sunlight and vapour and fast-flying shower. Fields nestle under it, and hills, and streams, and the dark-green woods, and the village with its homes and little gardens ; it sheds its benison impartially and most royally on them all. Did Noah think of this, when he and his were alone in that stripped and empty world, just emerging from desolation ? And was it his cordial and his reinforcement that, wherever he might go, God would remember to accompany him, and God's promise would not fail ? Certainly Christ puts the largeness of the heavenly grace, its catholicity and universality, beyond dispute. He is Son of Man as well as Son of Abraham, *a Samaritan* as truly as a Jew. To the manger the Magi came from the remote East, side by side with the shepherds from the near-by pastures of Bethlehem. On the Cross the title was written in the Greek and Latin of the West, no less than in the sacred Hebrew of law and prophecy and psalm. It is good to be confident that wherever, to Christian or to heathen listeners, at the gates of the sunrise or among

the lagoons and palms and corals of the sunset, the Gospel is spoken from a loving heart,
the power of the Lord is present to heal.
It is good to know that the differences which
divide men from each other are, for the
most part, of exceedingly slight importance
to the Saviour, Who overleaps the barriers
we make too frowning, and finds everywhere
the guests for His banquet and the heirs of
His redemption. There is a wise narrowness,
and we must not be so molluscous and in-
vertebrate that we shall dismiss as trifles
the verities which are essential. But there
is a wiser charity, and we must not magnify
God's " strictness with a zeal He will not
own." The arch of the rainbow is vast and
includes much.

III

Then, also, it predicates the completeness
of God's perfection.

It has seven colours, and together the
seven make up the unsullied and splendid
white. Righteousness and peace meet in
our God, and His severity is linked eternally
and inseparably with His goodness. On the

rainbow's outermost rim is the deep violet of divine power. Near the centre of its band is the azure blue of divine holiness. Farthest in is the burning red of divine love. Abraham and Moses, David and Isaiah, knew this manifold God. There are sentences of theirs in elucidation of Him, and in commendation, which outweigh what Plato and Bacon and Milton wrote; they move us more, and are more indispensable to our souls. But Christ teaches us best, and Christ crucified most prevailingly of all. We learn on Calvary the power of God; for He Who dies, apparently foiled, carries the great world's sin, and shakes off the hostile principalities and displays them as His conquest, and provides a redemption stronger than all the terrible kings that fight against man with " spears that are deadly bright,"

> Though out of the past they gather,
> Mind's Doubt and Bodily Pain;
> And pallid Thirst of the Spirit
> That is kin to the other twain;
> And Grief, in a cloud of banners,
> And ringletted Vain Desires,
> And Vice, with the spoils upon him
> Of me and my beaten sires.

We read at the Cross the holiness of God, far more vividly than in the mounting waters of the Flood or in the lightnings that consumed the cities of the plain ; so just and pure He is that there can be no pardon for guilty men until their sentence has been fully borne. And here we perceive the love of God for the unlovely. He smites the Good Shepherd instead of the wayward sheep ; and when He does so, His sword pierces His Own right hand as well as the Shepherd's heart : who shall say whether the Father's love or the Son's is the more ineffable and the more unbounded ? Violet of His power, blue of His holiness, and red of His love— this is the rainbow round about His throne. And the rainbow is nowhere seen so matchlessly as when we travel forth to the Hill of Reproach, to wonder, to mourn, to believe, and to adore.

IV

God's evangelist speaks yet again, to declare the timeliness of His comfort.

The beauty is set against a background of gloom. The vision comes to dissipate

the terror of the devouring waters, and to
end the long detention and imprisonment
of the ark. Vision and beauty are welcome
in themselves ; but they are thrice welcome
because they are granted in a seasonable
hour. They bring the message :—God is
nearest, He whispers His richest kindness,
He plans our noblest good, when our
sorrows abound, and when storm and pain
and loss brood over us. Once again, Christ
establishes and demonstrates the truth.
The Father, Who loved Him always, loved
Him supremely when He laid down His
life in the sinner's stead. The rainbow-
gospeller rang out its best tidings, when the
thunder-clouds hung lowest and deepest
over Golgotha. So we think of the Crucifixion as the sublimest and sweetest of paradoxes—triumph in helplessness and glory in
shame. " The convict's gibbet," a com-
mentator has said, " is the victor's car."
And let me, on my lower level and in my
smaller measure, make the utmost of the
high prerogative of suffering. God is
closest to me then, to baptize me into
patience and trust and courage, into in-

creasing purity, more earnest prayer, warmer consecration. I touch the print of my Lord's nails. I bear branded on body and spirit the marks of Jesus. Moses might tell his children, gathered about his knees, a story which ended in milk and honey, flocks and herds; but Christ tells me, His little child, the story which ends in a Cross. And thus He reminds me that I ought to be changed into the same Image.

Is the rainbow " still young and fine," as

> When Shem's admiring eye
> Its burnished flaming arch did first descry?
> When Terah, Nahor, Haran, Abram, Lot,
> The youthful world's grey fathers in one knot,
> Did with intentive looks watch every hour
> For its new light?

It should be. It is God's evangelist, with many things to say.

III

LOVE CAME DOWN ON SINAI

ELIJAH hoped that God would disclose Himself in the wind, or in the earthquake, or in the fire. The hope urged him to direct his steps to Horeb. He could not understand why the stroke of judgment lingered. He wished Jehovah to finish what had been begun on Carmel, and to consume every obstinate worshipper of Baal in the land. Therefore he fled to those frowning crags and peaks which, centuries before, had echoed with God's thunders and blazed with His lightnings. He longed for a second manifestation of the same conclusive and destructive power.

And there, at the hill of blackness and darkness and tempest, Elijah learned that God is Love. *A great and strong wind rent the mountains, and brake in pieces the rocks, but the Lord was not in the wind; and, after the wind, an earthquake, but the Lord was not*

*in the earthquake; and after the earthquake
a fire, but the Lord was not in the fire ; and
after the fire a still small voice* (1 Kings xix. 11,
12). Strange—was it not ?—that at Sinai,
and nowhere else, the prophet should discover that the tender mercies of God are
over all His works.

I

Wind, Earthquake, Fire, and the Voice ;
and the first three are ineffectual without
the last.

Nature, that is to say, gives no clear and
assuring knowledge of God. To the savage,
wood and lake and stream are peopled by
jealous forces, with eyes always watchful,
with memories that never forget, with
relentless arms. To Greeks long ago, trees,
rivers, and fields were crowded with deities,
and the common earth was an enchanted
ground ; minds so gifted, imaginations so
rare and delicate, discovered a romance at
each step, and journeyed from one fountain
of pleasure and marvel to another. Men of
science read us to-day many lessons of God's
wisdom and goodness from the phenomena

of the physical world. In the round ocean and the living air and the blue sky, in sunset touches and flower-bells, the poets discern the presence of Him Who besets us behind and before. It would be wrong, one perceives, to think of Nature as mute and dumb. Among its sights and sounds we may be perpetually recognizing the hem of God's garment, and we listen to the faint murmur and far-off whisper of Him. But without the Voice of the interpreting Word, of what saving value are these partial hints? They are suggestions; the Bible is revelation. They feel after the truth; it declares the truth. They bring us rumours of our Creator and King; it takes us by the hand, and conducts us to our Father, our Shepherd, and our Comforter. Wind, Earthquake, and Fire are not redemptive; they do not so commend God that we must love and obey Him. But let us hear the Voice— hear it for ourselves in the depths of our being; and they will have more authentic and constraining tidings to impart; they are His veritable spokesmen now, disclosing His character and sounding His praises as they never did before.

" A splintered rock, with an adder he had seen lurking below it, became the emblem of man's ruined nature, with the poison and the sting beneath. A single tree that crowned the top of a boulder amid the wreck of a fallen mountain showed where grace can rear its trophies. The reeds by the lochside bending to the sudden breeze called up the stir of the heart under the mysterious Spirit's breath. The wild ducks starting from the rushy covert, and in a moment out of reach, were the riches that fly away on wings. The little ruined church seen at the lower end of the lake was a symbol of the deserted shrine of the soul, on which Ichabod may be written." Thus Dr. John Ker, about Dr. Guthrie in his country home at Lochlee. Plainly, Thomas Guthrie had risen above Wind and Earthquake and Fire, to hearken to the Voice.

II

Wind, Earthquake, Fire, and the Voice; and God approaches nearer in each.

The Wind is in the spaces of the air,

invisible, mysterious. To it the element
of the elusive and the unaccountable, if not
of the wayward and capricious, belongs. It
is outside of me, and I can claim no intimacy
with it. The Earthquake is less distant,
directly underfoot, shaking my home and
myself. I am in no dubiety about the
Earthquake. The Fire is still more in-
dividually mine. I warm my hands at it,
and its glow is on my cheek. Perhaps its
sudden flame leaps out to seize and scorch
me. But the Voice draws nearest. It enters
my ear, with illumination for the mind, with
peace for the heart, with impulse and summons for the will. It conveys that which,
ever afterwards, must be part and parcel of
myself. Is there not here a parable of God's
gradual advances to the human soul ? The
general influences of His providence, the
play of circumstances, the surroundings of
our life, are the Wind which He sets blowing upon us, whose laws we cannot explain,
but whose movements, so far from being
haphazard, are designed and guided by Himself. The tremendous solemnities which
startle the world, tumult and war, far-spread

anxiety and multitudinous sorrow, are the Earthquake, meant to rouse us from worldliness and sleep, and to open wide our drowsy eyes into the wakeful certitude that this is not our rest. Then He comes closer. There are joys with which a stranger may not intermeddle, and which warm us like a flame. There is a furnace of temptation or of grief which others do not share. This is the Fire by means of which He seeks our truest well-being and our personal blessedness. But all of them are preparatory to the Voice, the living Word which the living Spirit accompanies. It penetrates to the inner citadel. It is spoken, as George Fox heard it speak, to our condition. It offers us the pardon of all our iniquities and the healing of all our diseases. It enriches us for time and eternity. To what ingenuities God has recourse ! What patience He displays ! With " unperturbed pace, deliberate speed, majestic instancy," the following Feet of the Hound of Heaven pursue their quarry. Let us give heed to Wind, Earthquake, and Fire, but chiefly to the Voice of His beseeching grace addressed to our very selves.

III

Wind, Earthquake, Fire, and the Voice; and three speak of judgment, but the fourth of mercy.

The Wind can woo. It can be soft and low.

> It may blow north, it still is warm;
> Or south, it still is clear;
> Or east, it smells like a clover farm;
> Or west, no thunder fear!

But often it is like Elijah's Wind, great and strong, rending the mountains and breaking the rocks in pieces, carrying its devastation over sea and land. Nor is it otherwise with the Earthquake. Even the slightest tremor of the solid ground is disquieting. It portends frightful possibilities, the upturning of what is homely and stable, the removal of landmarks we thought to be permanent. And if in a hundred instances the Fire is benefi-cent, it is calamitous in a hundred more. It is the instrument of ruin and loss as palpably as of life and comfort and help. This God of tempest, penalty, and death was the God Whose awful energies Elijah would have

c   25

had exemplified against the sinners of his country. And our God has these aspects. When a nation fills the cup of its pride and evil to the brim, when a church loses its first love, when a soul deliberately and perseveringly refuses Him, His holiness and His perfection compel Him to punish. But judgment is His strange work, to which nothing except necessity — a necessity infinitely sore to His heart—can ever drive Him. The Voice is God's real and consummate explanation of Himself; the Voice which is *a sound of gentle stillness*; the Voice which, though an Old Testament prophet heard it, and heard it on Sinai, is in essence the Voice of Christ and Calvary, " I am come not to condemn, but to save." There is no Lover like the God with Whom we have to do. He *hateth putting away*. He delights to bless.

IV

Wind, Earthquake, Fire, and the Voice; and, if the Voice itself starts with threatening, there is in it ever more and more of mildness and consolation.

The *sound of gentle stillness* has some stern things to say. It speaks of swords—Hazael's sword, and Jehu's, and Elisha's. But in the end its message is altogether kind. It tells the lonely man that he is not lonely, for God has still His witnesses and saints in idolatrous Israel. It clears away the clouds from Elijah's firmament, till he rejoices in the Lord of the Voice more than in the Lord he went out to see of Wind and Earthquake and Fire. So God's revelation of Himself to us may commence in power and in righteousness; but it mounts to and it terminates in love. We have an illustration in the Bible, where the magnificences of the Old Covenant precede the tendernesses of the New; and we fall on our faces before the Throne high and lifted up, ere we meet God at Bethlehem and Capernaum and Golgotha, our Brother, our Redeemer, our Friend. We have another proof in the conversion of the sinner. The Voice is a word of conviction first, awakening and alarming the conscience; and afterwards it is a word of full forgiveness. The Baptist preaches repentance, and then Jesus says to the bowed and broken spirit, *I will give you rest*. The author of *Grace Abounding* was like a ship beaten on the rocks, or like a drowning child in a mill pond, or like the manslayer at the gate of the City of Refuge with the avenger of blood at his heels. But, by and by, " comforting time was come "; and his Healer rang in his ears the strong consolations of God, " Thy sin is not unto death," and " I have loved thee with an everlasting love," and " Thy righteousness is in heaven," and " Christ is able "; and then all was well. We have the demonstration, no less, in the experience of the Christian. God searches you and me, chastens us, purges and disciplines us. His Voice brings trouble. But, whatever its accent is, there is no music of earth to compare with it; and its one desire is to lead us on to more holiness, more conformity to Christ, more fitness to accomplish His will here and to enter hereafter into His in-corruptible inheritance. When its purpose is achieved, it is a sound of gentle stillness indeed. All the pain has vanished now from the Voice. It communicates only a joy unspeakable and full of glory. We are in a garden better than Eden, and God walks and talks with us in the cool of the day.

IV

THE EYE IN THE HEART THAT LIES

HAS it ever occurred to you to reflect how very much the Bible says about the parts and organs of the body ? It makes mention of almost every limb and feature. Head and hands and feet, the breast and the back, and the five Gateways of Knowledge in the senses—they have each their memorial in God's Book. It is proof of the honour He puts on our bodies, and of the great future which He keeps for them. But one special reason His Word has for this frequency of reference. It employs the powers of the body to symbolize the endowments of the soul. From the material framework it reads us lessons regarding the deeper life which broods and beats within.

There is the eye. Men wonder at the miracle of it—its adaptability to its surroundings, the intricacy of its mechanism, its extraordinary sensitiveness, its eloquent expression of our thoughts and feelings. But, says God, there is a spiritual eye yet more remarkable. It is cleansed by the tears of penitence. It is lighted up by the steady lamp of trust. It gleams with the glow of hope. It radiates and diffuses the contagious warmth of love. Years do not dim its lustre. They brighten it. They make it surer and more clear-seeing.

Mine eyes are unto Thee, O God the Lord, one of the Psalmists sang (Psalm cxli. 8).

I

This eye looks inward.

It explores the profundities and abysses of that humanity of which it is part. No search, at first, is more disquieting and more humbling. It is a kind of Belgium — Belgium stripped and peeled — which the eye discovers. Instead of the wheat-laden fields, waste and desolation. Instead of happy homesteads, charred and forsaken ruins. Instead of a cathedral where God

31

is worshipped, the poor relics of a sanctuary which the barbarous enemy has profaned. A mind groping in the dark ; a conscience twisted and warped ; affections pulled downwards and chained to the earth ; the memory haunted by the regret that is close akin to remorse, and by the "dead things" that are "alive with a terrible might " ; the walls of the imagination hung with pictures that canker and corrupt—is not this a realm fatally out of joint, a land fair and fertile once but now impoverished and befouled ? And the desperate sadness of it all is intensified by the conviction of the soul that it is unable to remedy the mischief. Perhaps it recalls that grim Chinese apothegm, " There are two good men in the world, and one of them is dead, and the other is not born." It recalls the apothegm, and applies it to itself.

But *is* the other not born ? In innumerable instances he is, and he is growing daily in vigour. The eye of the Christian, looking within, begins to be aware of brighter elements in the situation. Its sorrows are alleviated. By and by they are counter-

acted and healed. For it perceives Some
One Who is at work among the plundered
fields, the orphaned homes, the outraged
churches—Some One Who wears the tran-
scendent and conquering name of the Spirit
of God. What cannot the Lord the Spirit
essay on our behalf ? and what will He not
perform ? He purifies the far-withdrawn
springs of motive. He creates and sustains
the heart in every thought renewed. A
famous writer of the last generation defined
God as " the Power not ourselves that makes
for righteousness." But the definition is
frigid. Power is not enough for us, if the
Power is neuter, and therefore unconscious,
unintelligent, and heartless. It is Personality
we want, masculine and mighty, motherly
and tender. And the eye is wonderfully
cheered and blessed which, gazing inward,
beholds a Paraclete, a Helper, an Advocate,
a Comforter, living and long-suffering and
loving, refusing to be driven away, staying
with us to the last to prevail over all the
craft and strength of the adversaries, and
to change the shadow of our death into the
morning. Gloriously and irresistibly He

makes for righteousness—He, not it. In the simplicity of faith let us go on trusting Him ; and the world within us will be a transfigured world.

II

The eye looks outward too.

It does not tire of the landscape of nature. Perhaps it has trained itself to some of the exactitudes of science. " Raise the stone," Jesus says in the Logion, " and there thou wilt find Me." And we raise the stone as the geologist does, to investigate its character, to determine its antiquity, to try and reconstruct that old, old universe of which it is the monument. Ah, and before we know, we are finding Christ afresh. Some good people are afraid of geology, as if its age-long cycles removed God to an immeasurable distance from themselves. But there is not a stone which should not carry us into the presence of our Lord. He fashioned it. He gave it its habitat and its history. He stirred in us the vision and faculty which can discern its significance. Or perhaps the eye prefers the method of open-orbed appreciation and frank enjoyment. " Cleave the wood," the Logion goes on, " and there am I." We cleave the wood, making our path over the grass and the pine-needles, marvelling at the great trees, gladdened by the choruses of the birds. And Jesus Christ is there. He still finds His text in the trees putting forth their tender leaves ; still condemns the tree and the man whose foliage is abundant and whose fruit is naught ; and still calls us to be branches in Himself, Who is the True Vine. So the Christian, whose eye is *unto thee, O God the Lord*, is perpetually catching a glimpse of his Master's vestments, and perpetually moving through a Holy Land. The rippling brook transports him to the River of the Water of Life, clear as crystal. The heathery hill in its September glory tells him of Christ's " dying crimson," and of the purple and kingly splendours in which he is himself being robed for Christ's sake. The landscape is sacramental.

As little does this eye tire of the study of man. Nature has its reverse side, which the disciple may not quite forget ; he hears the creation groan and travail in pain. But the contemplation of man is infinitely more poignant. That afflicts him with grief. What is worse, it plunges him in self-accusation and shame; for things would never have been so bad if he and his brethren had bestirred themselves. Yet to the Christian, man, when he is pettiest and smallest, when he is defiant and wicked, is nevertheless—what the man of Macedonia was to the apostle—*a vision*. He rouses consideration. He evokes wonder. He elicits sympathy and intercession and sacrifice. Four places convince me that man is, beyond doubt, a vision. The first is the Cradle of Bethlehem, where I find God so certain of man's essential worth that He enters his lot and becomes one with him in everything except his sin. The second is the Cross of Calvary, where I behold God so resolved to save man from his disability and death that He charges His Own holy Self with our manhood's curse. The third is the upper room on the Day of Pentecost, where I discover God so confident that man is capable of all grace and fruit-bearing that He condescends to dwell within him in divine illumination and power.

And the fourth is the Throne of the Majesty in the heavens, where I witness One Who is both God and Man reigning over the worlds, the Forerunner of men who believe in Him to-day and will sit beside Him to-morrow. To the spiritual eye man is never merely common, and never wholly repugnant. Always he is instinct with possibility. Always he is invested with pricelessness.

III

And the eye looks upward.

It is its favourite and accustomed direction. It is the quarter from which come its sunshine and summer, its hope and healing, its grace and mercy and peace. When it is occupied with what is within and what is without, it is constantly meeting God; how it exults that never and nowhere can it flee from Him ! But, times without number, its delight is to journey up, straight and swift, to Himself. It shuts out all the rest, and concentrates attention on God alone—God First and Last and Midst and without end.

I need to see Him forgiving me. The

37

enemy of my soul is quick and clever to insinuate doubts of my pardon. Therefore I
must return to look on the Lord my Healer,
on the Cross that was endured for me, and
on the Good Shepherd Who undertook my
forlorn and bankrupt cause. Dr. Chalmers's
Diary has many entries like the following :
" April 20th, 1840.—Began my first waking
minutes with a confident hold on Christ as
my Saviour. A day of great quietness " ;
and, " April 21st.—Let the laying hold of
Christ as my Propitiation be the unvary-
ing initial act of every morning " ; and,
" May 20th, 1841.—Why do I not go forth
both as a forgiven and as a vested creature,
forgiven all my trespasses and vested
with the righteousness of Christ ? " ; and
once again, " July 4th.—A pleasurable day.
Never am I in a better frame than when
dwelling in simple faith on Christ's offered
righteousness, and making it the object of
my acceptation." I have pleasurable days,
and days of great quietness, when I begin my
first waking minutes with a confident hold
on Christ as my Saviour, and when I dwell
in simple faith on His offered righteousness.

I need to see Him keeping me. The Psalmist was in dire straits. He has just said that he and his friends were like a derelict army, the bones of whose dead lay bleaching about the mouth of Sheol : it is the most melancholy of metaphors. But he recovers himself, and rises into a serener air. Over against the jubilant antagonists, and over against his own helplessness, he stations one sufficing Person. *But*—and all is well when we reach this But—*but our eyes are unto Thee, O God the Lord.* He who in every contingency and deadly risk, and these are thick as autumn leaves in Vallombrosa and as snowflakes in a December storm, is very sure of God ; he who cleaves to Him for the preservation of the life He has bestowed : his soul is delivered from death, his feet from falling, and his eyes from tears.

And I need to see Him perfecting me. Keeping is negative, to be safe-shielded from danger. Perfecting is positive, to grow steadfastly in wisdom and in holiness. What will secure it ? Eyes which always are turned to God our Lord. "With Thee on board," sings George MacDonald, "each sailor is a king." To live confiding in Him, and consulting Him, and loving all His words and all His ways, thus are we changed into His image, from glory to glory. Almightiness is above us, and Almightiness is within us ; and we crave nothing more.

V

A NONSUCH

OFTEN it is our profit and our delight to dwell on the completeness of Christ's kinship with ourselves. He is One of our company, bone of our bone, and soul of our soul. It is incontrovertible and blessed fact, and we do right to accentuate its lessons and to rejoice in its comforts. But there is an opposite fact, equally important, equally urgent. The Christ Who would vindicate us, delivering us from our enemies, and bringing us home to God, must needs stand quite alone. None is allied with Him in the dangers of His campaign or in the splendours of His victory. *Of the peoples*, He says, *there was no man with Me* (Isaiah lxiii. 3).

I

At the Manger Cradle we find one illustration of the solitariness. Miraculously, without ordinary fatherhood, He, apart from Whom we should be outcast and lost, took our nature for His Own—with no Father-hood except that of God, Whose Agent and Messenger the Holy Ghost was. Centuries beforehand it was written of Him, *Behold, a virgin shall conceive, and shall bear a Son, and shall call His name Immanuel.* This is an entrance into the world singular and unpre-cedented. Christ is alone, in the wonder of His humanity.

For indeed a humanity which is without parallel, and beyond compare, follows the extraordinary birth. It is raised far above our fragmentariness ; perfect at each of its stages and in each of its aspects, as child and boy and youth and man, as worker and suppliant and sufferer and conqueror; joining in concord what, in our one-sidedness, we suppose must be contradictories—mercy and truth, goodness and severity, action and rest ; catholic, so that it outgoes every narrowness, overleaps every barrier of sex or class or nation or epoch, is at home in every age and beneath every sky. And this is the least of it, no more than the suburbs

and outcourts of the Wonder; we are not
yet in the inner shrine. Christ's humanity
is without spot, and untouched by our con-
tamination and evil. The long entail of
sin is broken at last. One born of a woman
is, even as Man, free from man's disobedience and transgression, from wandering or
the wish to wander, from all loose and un-
governed movements of the soul, from any
will except the will of God. When the
prince of this world comes, as he will come
both before and after the Temptation in
the wilderness, he finds nothing in our
Lord. And the amazing negative im-
plies a greater and more dazzling positive.
Christ's humanity is dedicated to God, is
filled into all the fullness of God, is at one
with God from centre to circumference
and from first to last. We have to be
reintroduced to God after absence and
distance, revolt and rebellion. But His
thought and love never leave the Father's
house, and the Father is the passion of His
heart those three-and-thirty years. Thus
He comes, with none to help or uphold,
matchless and alone.

We need the undefiled humanity of our Saviour. Had any limitation or selfishness or sin clung to Him, it must have disqualified Him fatally for redeeming us. But the sight of His perfection, while it is the condemnation of what we are, is the assurance of what in Him we are becoming. A friend wrote me a year or two since about a spring-time in Switzerland. "Among the Jura," he said, " I waded one day for five miles through myriads of wild daffodils with big blue gentians interspersed. It was the most gorgeous spectacle I ever beheld, and suggested the words, *Eye hath not seen the things which God hath prepared for them that love Him.*" Indeed, eye has not seen the marvel of the spring-time which the Lord Jesus Christ gives. He banishes the last vestiges of ice and snow. He carpets the soil of our wintry souls with yellow gold and celestial blue, till we cannot "but be gay in such a jocund company," and all our

> heart with pleasure fills,
> And dances with the daffodils.

He conforms our humanity to His Own.

II

On the Road between Olivet and Jerusalem we have a second illustration of
Christ's aloneness. What do we read of
the charger which carries our Monarch on
the day of His triumph ? This, that it is
a colt whereon never man sat. A common
farmyard beast, and yet fitted for its thrice-
honourable and thrice-sacred task, since it
has borne no one until it bears the Prince of
the kings of the earth ; it has kept itself for
Him. We look at it, and we think of the
singularity and miracle of His kinghood.

For this is royalty without a trace of
pretension and parade. Its grandeurs are
not unveiled except to eyes which God has
purged and couched into harmony with
Christ's judgments and affections. We
lavish applause on high station, on forceful-
ness and initiative, on genius and success.
He keeps His love for the poor and contrite,
the simple, the men and women who are as
little children ; they are like Himself, meek
and lowly in heart. None the less, this is
royalty which makes limitless and unrivalled

demands. Christ asks, and deserves, and in innumerable instances receives a service which the absolutism of Cæsar or Napoleon would never dare to seek. It pierces to the imagination and the motive. It rules us through the week as inexorably as on the Holy Day. It calls for every power of the soul, the mind, the body. It survives death, and runs on through all eternity. Mr. Arthur Shearly Cripps delineates St. Paul— " Knight of the Cross, the Nails, the Lance, Priest of theophanies of pain." He sees the quarterings on his shield—" Rome's sword, and Sion's scourge, Philippi's rods, and Lystra's stone." He remembers his toil,

> Who, teaching Troas all a night,
> For Assos strode with earliest day

He is shamed by the thoroughness and the selflessness of his devotion—

> He sailed in dreams an Argonaut,
>   A Seamless Coat his Fleece of Gold;
> A war-worn voyager, he freed
>   Sheep fast within the giant's fold.

These are the demands of our King. They are beyond comparison great, but not a whit too great for Him to make. Yes, and this is royalty whose benefactions are munificent. Happy are Christ's men, happy His servants who stand continually before Him. They hear His wisdom. They know His indwelling strength. They are heirs of His grace and mercy and peace. His right arm brings them salvation ; and the salvation widens and deepens, expands and multiplies, the longer they are familiar with it.

A kinghood so meek and so spiritual, so interminable and so searching, so wealthy and so generous, is Christ's alone. But it is our joy and our life, here and hereafter, to be in subjection to it and to Him.

III

Beside the Grave in Joseph's garden we discover a third illustration of Christ's unapproachableness. They *laid Him in a tomb that was hewn in stone, wherein never man had yet lain.* It has welcomed no previous tenant. It is new. That, also, is in accordance with the fitness of things. The garden grave preaches the solitude, the pre-eminence, and the glory of His death.

All men die. If death is a stupendous solemnity, it is, viewed from another angle, a trite and hackneyed commonplace.

> Pallida mors æquo pulsat pede pauperum tabernas,
> Regumque turres.

But no man has died like Christ. Consider the essential improbability—impossibility, we had almost said—of His death. Godhead is joined with manhood in Him; and it is the strangest of strange happenings that God should die. We cannot fathom it. Perforce, we stand about a stone's-cast off. Vaguely and dumbly we feel what self-abnegation and what love are here. Consider the unshackled freedom of His death. We go, because we must. He went, because He would. His heart was in that awful crucifixion outside the gate. His will willed it, not through His brief earthly ministry merely, but from His eternal past : He is the Lamb slain in purpose and intention from the foundation of the world. He lays down His life spontaneously, generously,

as a Priest does, as a Prince does. In the
Latin Father's phrase, He is both Victim and
Victor. Consider the unplumbed sorrow
of His death. Death has its sadness always,
if not for those who are gone into the world
of light, then for these who sit lingering
here; it never fails to drape some hearts
in black. But our sadness, when it is most
shattering, is not to be mentioned in the
same breath with His. Christ's is the grief
of the Holy One round Whom the sins of the
chief of sinners accumulate and gather. It
is the orphanhood of the Perfect Son Who
passes out, bearing our iniquities, into a
darkness where even the face of the Father
is hidden. The sounding-lead of strongest
thought, simplest faith, deepest penitence,
warmest love, has never touched, nor ever
will, the bottom of these seas. But consider, too, the unmeasured harvests of His
death. Many deaths are fruitful — the
soldier's, maintaining the good name of his
country, and guarding her liberties " at
life's dear peril "; the martyr's, witnessing
to truth on the scaffold; the missionary's,
whose sepulchre claims the heathen soil for

49

his Master Christ. But Christ's Own death bears fruit more inexhaustible. All sons and daughters in the family of God; all holy men and women; all ambassadors of the King, whose testimony and labour are compelling the deserts to blossom as the rose; all citizens of the New Jerusalem who have washed their robes and made them white in the blood of the Lamb, and who, as Rabbi Duncan said, are " prouder of the redness than the whiteness "—these are its harvest. God grant we owe everything which is most precious in time, and most desirable in eternity, to the Corn of Wheat Which fell into the ground and died on Mount Calvary.

In death, as in birth and in life, there is none of the peoples with Christ. Alone He bears the shame, and finishes the work. Alone He returns from the fight, travelling in the greatness of His strength. Alone He brings you and me the salvation which cost Him all but costs us nothing, and which is full and present and everlasting.

VI

THE WORD THAT IS THE SYMBOL OF MYSELF

THREE times—no oftener—the name "Christian" occurs in the New Testament. The friends of Jesus did not themselves employ it. They got it from outsiders, who had no personal share in their secret, and who did not walk their path. It shows us the infant Church as it appeared to its critics—critics always observant, generally unsympathizing, not seldom resolute in opposition and hostility. We may well ask ourselves whether we leave on a keen-eyed world the same impressions.

I

The disciples were called Christians first in Antioch (Acts xi. 26). There is the wealth of a Christian.

Men and women to whom "The Christ" was watchword and talisman, food and comfort and strength, sunshine and dew : this was what the heathen townsfolk of Antioch discovered in these saints of the first century. They coined for them the sobriquet of "the Christians," because, so patently, so obviously, the feeble folk could not dispense with their Christus. He was the Crest on their flag, the Beacon flashing from their hilltop, the Polestar in their sky. Well, it was a clever nickname ; and probably the citizens laughed as they fastened it on the eccentric Nazarenes. They took credit for hitting them off neatly and sententiously, with piquancy and point. But, more than once, a nickname has been a tribute, a panegyric, and a diadem of honour ; and here is an instance when it was signally so. Cicero crowns Antioch with the superlative *nobilissima* ; and, in simple fact, the city rose to its noblest, when it garlanded Christ's bondmen with its jest. For the jest was a real dignity, a splendid truth, a wreath which God Himself wove for the brows of those whom He dearly loved.

But about ourselves. " Le nom," says
Renan, writing about this very incident,
" est le signe définitif de l'existence.
C'est par le nom qu'un être individuel ou
collectif devient lui-même." And is the
name " Christian " the symbol and summa-
tion of our existence ? By it do we reach,
and recount, and publish to all and sundry,
our selfhood, our identity, the marrow and
quintessence of our being ? Does our
wealth so evidently reside in Christ—Christ
dying, living, teaching, pleading, reigning,
returning—that men notice the fact, and
talk about it, and single us out for their
banter because of it ? If it does, we can
afford to face the banter ; for we hold the
treasure which is inestimable. Our beliefs
—they should not be orthodox so much as
Christ-possessed and Christ-centred. Not
of atonement in the abstract are we to speak,
so often as of Him Who loved us and gave
Himself for us ; not of faith, but rather of
Him Whom we believe, and Who keeps that
which we have committed to Him ; not of
sanctification, nearly so much as of Him
Whose very life beats and pulses behind and

beneath our life; not of immortality, but of Him Who will come again to receive us to Himself, that where He is we may be with Him. And our practice—it should not be a compliance with a dead code, even if the code embodies the mind and will of the King of kings; and it should not be a painstaking discharge of duty, even if the duty is enacted by the heavenly Master. Quicker and more delightful it ought to be; because it is a daily walk where we see the very footmarks of Christ going in front of us, a daily sensitiveness lest we grieve His gracious heart, a daily fellowship with One Who is all our Desire. Yes, are we Christians, because the Christ Himself is our wealth? And do those who watch us, in friendliness or in unfriendliness, draw this conclusion and pronounce this verdict?

II

With but little persuasion thou wouldest fain make me a Christian (Acts xxvi. 28). There is the hunger of a Christian.

In himself, he is at rest and at home.

His heart is full to overflowing. He sits at a royal banquet. But, into the home and the heart and the banqueting-hall, the thought pursues him of the poverty and famine of men unacquainted with his feast of fat things. He understands Samuel Rutherfurd's intensity of longing, when they banished him from Anwoth. " O, if I might but speak to three or four herdboys of my worthy Master, I would be satisfied to live in any of Christ's basest outhouses." He is of one mind with Richard Baxter, when the Act of Uniformity threw him and many who were of kindred spirit with him out of their parishes. " Could we but go among Turks and heathens, and speak their language, I should be but little troubled for the silencing of eighteen hundred ministers at once in England." Or he is like Paul before Agrippa. The king tries to ward off the apostle's earnestness with a flippant word. " Do you suppose that in so short a time, and with arguments so flimsy, you will coax me into becoming *a Christian*, the votary of a sect which is everywhere spoken against, the adherent and advocate of a

55

puerile heresy ?" The impassioned preacher has frightened Agrippa, and he shelters himself behind a sneer, and hastens to escape from one who looks as if he would take no denial.

But we are too otiose, too futile, too easily alarmed by rebuff, and too little enamoured of aggressiveness and zeal. On fire with the craving to gain others for Christianity and Christ!—it is the last thing which our neighbours are likely to say of us, and the last thing which our custom-bound and comfort-loving hearts wish to be true of ourselves. Yet we know the penury and peril of the life that is ignorant of the Saviour, how it starves in a land of sand and thorns, and how it hastens down to darkness and the second death. We know too that Christ is what this life requires, and that only when it falls into His kind arms will it be safe and well. And we know that the time is shortened, and the night impends. How can we sit still ? Necessity should be laid on us. Love should force us out from the warm hearth and the overflowing feast to where, in cold and gloom and want, our kinsfolk pine and die. In our conversation, by our character, through our intercessions and prayers, we ought to be persuading these sisters and brothers of ours to become such as we are.

That is an exquisite page of *Eothen*, in which Mr. Kinglake describes his approach to Egypt. For eight days he had been in the Desert, the flaming sky above him, the sand below him glaring with light and fire. But on the eighth day a dark line appeared on the forward horizon, and soon the line deepened into a fringe sparkling as if sown with diamonds. Before him at length were the gardens and minarets of Egypt, and the mighty works of the Nile. That evening, for the last time, his tent was still pitched in the Desert. But one of his Arabs stalked away rapidly towards the west, without telling him of his errand. After a while he returned. He had toiled on a graceful service. He had travelled all the way on to the border of the living world, and he brought his master back for a token an ear of rice, full, fresh, and green. " An ear of rice, full, fresh, and green "—why are we not taking it from our living world to the dwellers in the Desert ? God make us ashamed that we have been laggards too long ! God stir in us the Christian's inextinguishable hunger !

III

If a man suffer as a Christian, let him glorify God in this name (1 Peter iv. 16). There is the cross of a Christian.

By the time that St. Peter wrote his Epistle, the world, Jewish and pagan, had wakened up to the conviction that, if Christ should have His way, much which it prized would be undermined, and discredited, and driven clean out of the knowledge and practice of men. It ceased to be a jesting and tolerant world. It became angry. It commenced to annoy, to thwart, and to persecute " the panting huddled flock whose crime was Christ." These were days when a man might *suffer as a Christian*—wild wintry days of biting sleet and hail. And soon the enemies would be girding Peter himself, and carrying him to his crucifixion ;

would be leading Paul from his dungeon, to die under the headsman's axe on the road to Ostia ; would fling Ignatius to the wild beasts in the Roman amphitheatre ; would send white-haired Polycarp to the flames in Smyrna. He who means to wear the appellation of Christian in those surroundings will need to be strong and of a good courage. Rather let us say, he will need to cast himself on Christ in the simplicity of an unreserved faith. Then the Lord, Whose Own Cross was incomparably heavier, will enable him to lift his lesser cross, and to kiss its wood and nails and ignominy and pain.

Does anybody suffer as a Christian nowadays ? Undoubtedly, as Uganda and China and Armenia will testify. But among ourselves ? Surely ; although the furnace may not blaze with such a white and unrelenting heat. If in business I refuse to countenance any method which Christ cannot approve, and am counted a fool for my scrupulosity ; if in society there are amusements from which I must hold aloof, and they stigmatize me as morose and hypocritical ; if I am compelled by a keen-edged conscience and a punctilious heart to defend my Master when He is defamed, and then am ridiculed for my witness ; if the element of sacrifice enters perceptibly and undisguisedly into my religion : I bear the Christian's reproach, and climb the Christian's thorny and blessed hill. And let me *glorify God in this name*. Let me carry the name, not with bated breath and whispered humbleness, but as a high distinction and most gracious ornament. Unquestionably, He will have His strange glad succours for me, and the way of the Cross will be the way of Light. I shall fare as Robert Browning's martyr did :

> I was some time in being burned ;
> But at the close a Hand came through
> The fire above my head, and drew
> My soul to Christ.

And then I shall " forget it all "—the pitying smile of patronage, the sharp shaft of sarcasm, the hot flame of fierce antagonism and dislike.

Sometimes, in the early years, people were so ignorant of Christ that they mispronounced His name, turning " Christus " into " Chrestus," and " Christianus " into

" Chrestianus." One almost imagines that there was a heavenly inspiration in the mistake. For " Chrestus " and " Chrestianus " mean benign, benevolent, humane, unselfish, kind. Because we exult in the Christian's wealth, and have no rest from his hunger, and are welcoming his cross with a ready mind, may you and I, through all the future, be more than conventional Christians —may we be manifest Chrestians.

VII

THE POWERS OF PENTECOST

WAS not Joel, the son of Pethuel, a happy man? In the goodly fellow-ship of the prophets none could say more explicitly and decisively than he, " I believe in the Holy Ghost." He had distinct and satisfying foreglimpses of the blessedness of the latter day. He had his Pentecost in advance. This was God's oracle through his lips, *It shall come to pass afterward that I will pour out My Spirit upon all flesh* (Joel ii. 28).

I

Joel sees the largeness of the Spirit's love. He is certain that, when His era dawns, the Lord the Spirit will surmount our separat-ing walls, and will be free from every ex-clusiveness and every prejudice. There will

be an untrammelled catholicity about Him.
There will be a wideness like that of the
sun and the sea. On whom is He to descend?
On *all flesh*. At His touch the barriers of
nationality crumble. Jew and Gentile are
equally dear to that capacious heart. Britain,
with her long centuries of privilege, is not
His care to the neglect of other lands;
China, India, and Africa are as priceless in
His eyes. The prophet expands the thought
of this universality. *Sons and daughters* are
visited by the Spirit. He enters the sphere
of the family to sweeten and sanctify it.
Old men and young men are taught His
supernal knowledge. He prizes both the
experience of age and the enthusiasm of our
earlier years, and He has His divine uses for
both. *Servants and handmaids* utter His word
and do His will. The humblest fulfil His
errands and win His triumphs more certainly
and more conqueringly than those who pride
themselves on wealth or social position or
the churchly ordination of men. After all,
it is impossible to cabin and confine the
best possessions. A fair landscape belongs
to everybody who looks on it with a heart

which appreciates its sublimity and beauty. A good book is not restricted to one epoch of time or to one class in the community. Twentieth-century children can " speak the tongue that Shakespeare spoke." Cavaliers and conservatives, when they know what is good for them, hold the faith and morals " that Milton held." So it is with the grace of the Spirit. He laughs at limitations. He is the Wind blowing where it lists. He is the Water breaking out in refreshment where we least expect it. He is the Fire kindling ten thousand times ten thousand souls into heat and heartsomeness. Let these boundless sympathies be our encouragement. There is room in them for us, whoever and whatever we may be, and, if we ask Him, He will not say us Nay. But let them be our reproof also. For we are apt to be jealous of irregular movements in religion, and of unauthorized speakers and workers, when we should be much more afraid of fighting against the Holy Ghost. His Jerusalem is a *town without walls, for the multitude of men therein*. His charities have no east or west or north or south. The love of the Spirit is liberal and large.

II

Joel sees, too, the variety of the Spirit's endowment.

There are diversities of operations. There are many-coloured gifts. The energy has no uniform and stereotyped development. The music has a hundred chords. Frequently, Joel says, the presence of the Spirit is disclosed in *prophecy*. Let Him anoint and control us, and our lips are opened. We have the skill and the will to publish the truth concerning our Saviour and King. We speak with new tongues, the tongue that warns, the tongue that invites, the tongue of earnest and persuasive appeal, the tongue of irrepressible joy and singing. A burden of the Lord is laid upon us, and we are not able to keep silence. And that is a state of things greatly to be coveted among Christian men and women to-day, who are much too reticent, and in awe of their neighbours, and afraid lest they should offend against the conventions and the proprieties. Would that the time were indeed come, " wherein Moses, the great prophet, may sit in heaven rejoicing to see that memorable and glorious wish of his fulfilled, when not only our seventy elders but all the Lord's people are become prophets"! Or just as frequently, Joel affirms, the presence of the Spirit is disclosed in *dream*. He begets the vastest hopes. He fosters the expectation of the harvests which are sure to be. That, no less, is what the Church and the disciple need. We yield too easily to depression. We despair of our own perfecting, and of the onward and indomitable march of Christ's kingdom. But the Holy Ghost is not dead ; He lives, and He must prevail. If we hearken to Him, He will teach us to dream of marvels, apocalypses, exultations, years of the right hand of the Most High ; and the dreams He awakens are not utopian fancies—they are facts which approach nearer hour after hour. Yes, and frequently, writes Joel, the presence of the Spirit is disclosed in *vision*. Then, like the captain of Israel long ago, we live as "seeing the invisible." Then we think and speak, and conduct our business, and talk with our children and friends, and move

through the streets, all the time *sub specie
æternitatis*. Our real universe is the universe hidden from sight. We walk with
God. We abide in Christ. We are citizens
of the Holy Land. Perhaps this is the most
desirable endowment of all. For the men
and women who " by the Vision splendid
are on their way attended " are the men and
women who glorify their Lord, who continually do good, and who win souls. May
you and I be of that enviable and excellent
company !

III

And Joel sees the magnificence of the
Spirit's power.

As he studies it, the power is terrible.
It is majestic, but it is ominous and over-
whelming. He hears God speak of *wonders
in the heavens and in the earth*; and the
recital follows of portents which arrest and
alarm—the blood-red sky, the pitiless sun,
the columns of sand and dust which the
sirocco raises high in the air. Do not let
us forget that the Spirit can be minister
of the divine severities as of the divine

67

gentlenesses. He is Himself in thorough harmony with God's enmity against sin and God's unbending righteousness; and, when the law of holiness is persistently set aside, His voice is a dreadful voice. Yet His wonders, even when they are fearful, may be, and are usually meant to be, the precursors of life and peace.

Beneficent streams of tears flow at the finger of pain,
And out of the cloud that smites beneficent rivers of rain.

Take it on the large scale, and the Spirit has something to do with the seething tumult of war. These upheavals, these miseries, the blood and the fire and the pillars of smoke, are meant by Him to lead the nations to Christ, Who alone can rectify their wrongs and satisfy their hearts. Or take it on the small scale, and how often the Spirit has prefaced the conversion of a sinner, and the restoration of a backgoing disciple, and the filling of a saint into all the fullness of God, by contrition and penitence, by tempest and weeping! Through the midnight He conducts us to the morning, and to the tasks in which He has most

68

pleasure—His healing, uplifting, transfiguring tasks. In one aspect of it or in another, the magnificence of the Spirit's power is our clamant want in these days. We have in the Church an abundance of light and knowledge, of ingenuity and resourcefulness. But the Power which is not to be discredited or checked or turned back, which sweeps the stoutest obstacles away, which summons the prisoners into liberty, which compels the deserts to rejoice and blossom as the rose, for this let us importune our God till He sends it to us.

IV

Lastly, Joel sees the efficacy of the Spirit's prayer.

In the golden year of the Holy Ghost, *it shall come to pass that whosoever shall call on the name of the Lord shall be delivered.* The Spirit is Inspirer of prayer. He impels us to call, and qualifies us so to call that the answer descends, sure, seasonable, full. To Him we owe the sharp sense of poverty which drives us to the Storehouse of supply.

By Him we are kept from presenting requests, foolish or superficial or impatient, which are at variance with the counsel of God. He reveals Christ and makes Him all our Boast, so that we lean solely on our Redeemer's death and our High Priest's intercession. He creates and deepens the conviction of the plenitude of the Lord with Whom we plead, until we feel that Infinity without a bottom and without a shore is the ocean from which we draw. Let His breath pervade the place of prayer, and our communion will no more be an effort, a vexation, and a penance ; it will be a sunrise, an outrush of the living waters, a capture of heaven itself and heaven's unsearchable riches. Whosoever calls thus on the name of the Lord shall be delivered, irrefutably, beyond expectation, not to the half of the kingdom which is unseen and eternal, but to the whole. Whether the blessedness we crave is for ourselves, or for the Church of Jesus Christ, or for a world so much of which lies in the shadow of death, God the Spirit in us is seeking the same thing—seeking it *with groanings which cannot be uttered* ; and

THE POWERS OF PENTECOST

His wish and our wish will have an over-flowing reward. He asks, and we receive. He knocks, and it is opened to us.

I believe in the Holy Ghost—who can estimate how much it means ?

VIII

LET'S TRUDGE ANOTHER MILE

NO good shepherd would fold his sheep on a dusty high-road or on a bleak and burnt mountain-summit. But see what God says of the members of His flock : *They shall feed in the ways, and their pastures shall be in all high places* (Isaiah xlix. 9). The miracle is impossible in the world of Nature. It is of regular occurrence in the world of Grace.

I

So here is a benediction for the week-day of work.

Perils haunt the week-day. We may be engrossed by our labour. We may be worried by the multitude of cares it awakens. It masters us. The dust of the ways along which our feet must plod invades our spirit, to cover what is more ethereal, and to hurt our best life. " Late and soon, getting and spending, we lay waste our powers " ; and the unseen and the eternal run the gravest risk of being forgotten. But there is a transfiguration for the week-day. *They shall feed in the ways*, the text declares. They shall be nourished by the pressure. They shall glean help from the common round, and the incessant demands, and the little duties that win no praise from men. These things prove our religion. Are we doing them from the great motives, to please Christ, and to commend His Kingdom ? It is a sure criterion of the reality of our faith. It is an Ithuriel's spear to unmask whatever is unworthy ; and " no falsehood can endure its touch of celestial temper." They conduct us directly into God's Presence. Our continual need of wisdom, patience, kindliness, hope, as we face their requirements, is just His continual invitation to draw near, that He may do exceeding abundantly above what we ask. And they give us a store of sustaining memories. It is in the week-days that we accumulate

F   73

most of our recollections of the goodness
of our Lord. How we looked to Him, and
were lightened. How we obeyed Him, and
found His promise faithful and true. How
we ventured everything for Him, and had
everything restored to us twice over. These
are green meadows and quiet waters to discover on the stony roadsides.

If we would feed in the ways, where there
are many coming and going, and the calls
upon us are crowded and exacting, one thing
we must remember—to halt for an instant
every now and then, that we may look up
to God, and may cast our burden on Him.
That is essential, but nothing more than that.
Then we shall go forward revived and in-
vigorated. Then our deepest life will thrive
in the throng and the grime of our toil. The
great Bishop of Hippo, and teacher of the
Church universal, has a famous saying about
the Lord's Supper : *Crede et manducasti*,
" Believe, and thou hast eaten." But you
and I may turn it round and say, *Labora et
manducasti*, " Work, and thou hast eaten."
For there is truth in this version too. There
is a viaticum to sustain our souls.

74

II

And here is a solace for the heaviness of sorrow.

The word grows stronger and richer as it travels on. *Their pastures shall be in all bare heights*, God tells us next. And if it is good to have a table spread on the beaten highways, it is better to have springing grass up among the wild crags, where the eye of sense sees not a bite for the starving sheep. It is a declaration that the man is favoured whom the Lord afflicts, and that His chastening is designed to yield peaceable fruit of righteousness. Experience justifies trial. Ten thousand saints are ready to testify that their periods of most rapid and unmistakable spiritual growth have been their periods of trouble. The winter accomplishes more than the summer for the soul's development and advance. The valley of weeping is a well of living waters, and the barren heights are a dewy and pleasant field. And grace prepares trial—the grace of our Saviour, our Leader, our Lover. He has been in the cold and frost before us, and He will take care that our winter is not nearly so keen as His Own. His made His heart bleed; it slew Him outright; ours, through His wise and tender tuition, will instruct us, brace us, ripen us into His likeness. Christ is never busier within our natures than when we are out from the shelter, and away from the plenty, on the chill hilltops. And faith welcomes trial. It does not start difficulties. It does not rebel. It bows its head and worships. It had rather sojourn with Abraham, where it must be fed with God's hidden manna, than sit with Lot in the gate of the city, where there are cattle and money and the applause of men and a famine-stricken and hungry heart.

What ails Mr. Thomas Hardy that, even when his singing robes are on him, he is so uniformly chill and sombre, his skies always grey, and his winds a shivering and arctic cold? Life for him has a " sad seared face," and he wearies of seeing her and her "draggled cloak."

> But canst thou not array
> Thyself in rare disguise,
> And feign like truth, for one mad day,
> That Earth is Paradise?

How good it would be for Mr. Hardy, with those wonderful powers of his, to be a little child in God's house ! He would still find sadness crossing Life's face, but, behind the sadness, he would read in the face an abiding trust and calm. And he would not want to feign that Earth is Paradise, because he would know that it is not and cannot be ; his would be the more satisfying confidence that Earth and trial are a stage on the ascent to Paradise and an education for its rest and joy. A friend told me once of a naval officer who, on a stormy day, went in a submarine down into the waters of the North Sea, and heard the pebbles churning and rasping at the bottom, and realized that it was as tempestuous there as on the surface. But the North Sea is comparatively shallow. Dive into the Atlantic or the Pacific, and you will come to a central depth, where the agitations have ceased, and which is still but not stagnant. When our faith penetrates far enough, it never finds fault with God. It reposes undismayed in His good and acceptable and perfect will. In the jagged corries and on the rocky cliffs we discover His full feast.

III

Here, once again, is a glory for the hour of death.

To our senses and our affections death is repellent. We have as little inherent liking for it as the sheep and lambs have for the arid ways and the naked heights. The feeling is inevitable; but in Christian souls it is frequently carried to unreasonable lengths. We study death overmuch from the earthward side; let us contemplate it from the heavenward, and it is altered completely. We shrink from the ways, but God bids us reflect that they lead us and ours to where we shall follow the Lamb whithersoever He goeth. We distrust the sternness of the mountains, but this is His word: *Upon the mountains shall their fold be, and there shall they lie in a good fold.*

Mrs. Browning—more believing than Mr. Hardy—has a poem, which she calls "The Fourfold Aspect." It is about the different conceptions we cherish of death. First, there is the child's fantasy. You tell him of those lying in the churchyard till the last trump

78

rouses them; and it is "a tale of fairy-ships with a swan-wing for a sail": so carelessly he thinks upon the dead. Next, there is the youth's picture. He associates with the men of long ago, heroes with the laurel, poets with the bay, Achilles and Ulysses, Arthur and Roland; and to him death is a Valhalla, where

> none can enter in
> Far below a paladin:

so royally he thinks upon the dead. Then there is the sufferer's dirge. The funeral is at his gate; his tears are falling; his wail goes up, " Dost Thou see then all our loss, O Thou agonized on Cross ? "—so mournfully he thinks upon the dead. But, lastly, there is the Christian's victory. The angels predict "Sabbath hours at hand," and, better still, Christ is with His disciple.

> He stands brightly, where the shade is,
> With the keys of Death and Hades.

So, hopefully, quietly, triumphantly, the Christian thinks upon the dead.

Wherefore, let us be always confident. In Christ, we feed sumptuously in the ways, and our pastures are lush and wholesome on all bare heights.

IX

PRESERVE THE SEAL UNSULLIED

CLEMENT of Rome, whose name is in the Book of Life, tells us of a saying of the Lord which the Gospels do not commemorate, " Keep the flesh pure, and preserve the seal unsullied." Whether or no the words fell in this actual form from the lips of Him Whom we greet as Master, they enshrine the desire and injunction of Christ for His servants. That apostle who has interpreted His mind with a divine clearness and decision corroborates their teaching when he writes, *I beseech you, brethren, that ye present your bodies a living sacrifice* (Romans xii. 1). A body carried to the altar, and continually yielded in dedication to God—it is the proper thank-offering, and the reasonable service, of the Christian. But perhaps we are a little surprised at the emphasis which is laid on the physical side of our nature. It may seem as if a lower gift were being sought from us, than if we had been counselled to bring the intellect with its thoughts, or the imagination with its lights and shades, or the will with its determinations, or the heart with its intensity of warm attachment, or the deep and meditative spirit with its power of penetrating far into that world which is unseen and eternal. Yet St. Paul selected his word most wisely.

I

For there is a warning here against a divorce which is often made.

Men and women pretend that the inner sanctuary of life is yielded up to God, while they keep its outer courts for their own pleasure and sin. Our faith and our love, we protest, we have freely devoted to Christ and to heaven; but the members, the appetites, and the activities of the body we retain still for ourselves; we can use them, and gratify them, much as we

81

choose. Historians describe old St. Paul's, the cathedral which preceded Sir Christopher Wren's stately edifice, and which perished with so much else in the Great Fire of London. It was exceedingly long, occupying a large space in the centre of a busy city ; and it came to be regarded almost as a public thoroughfare. Men walked up and down its aisles and corridors, talking of the markets and the news of the day. "The noise in it," said Bishop Earle, "is like that of bees, a strange humming mixed of tongues and feet; it is a kind of still roar or loud whisper." And, in the midst of the tongues and feet, stood the pulpit with the preacher in it, trying vainly to compete with interests and fascinations which were too strong for him. The "still roar" drowned his arguments. The "loud whisper" rendered nugatory and barren his most eager persuasions and appeals. It is how some of us are tempted to divide the church and temple of our being. God can have the pulpit ; but we want to reserve the floors and passages for our own purposes and likings. That is a separation not only incongruous in itself, and in hundreds of disastrous instances attended with fatal issues in character, but totally futile and impossible. God will never be contented with belief and emotion, if the body is held back from Him, and is permitted to follow anything which is unworthy or questionable. He demands the unbroken personality, demands it all as He deserves it all. Let each of us be quite sure that He rules Eargate and Eyegate and Mouthgate, as utterly and imperiously as He rules the centre and citadel of Mansoul.

II

But there is also a picture here of a tribute which is voluntary and entire.

The sacrifice is that of the body; but really it is the whole manhood which offers the sacrifice. Mind and soul are behind the scenes, invisible but operative; they are the white-robed and reverential priests, bearing the gift to the altar, and making it God's inviolable possession. The gift would not be worth having otherwise.

Suppose that an external force dragged the body to services and sanctities from which thought and volition and affection stood aloof, uninterested and sullen spectators : what graciousness or value could such a coerced obedience claim ? It would be something which our Lord must reject— something hard and slavish and repugnant in which He could detect no charm. You remember that great day on Mount Moriah, when Abraham built the cairn, and laid the wood upon it, and bound his only son Isaac whom he loved, and lifted the priestly knife to slay his child. It was the readiness of both father and son to embrace God's piercing and yet holy will which invested the momentous transaction with its spiritual significance. Abraham's soul moved his arm to inflict the death-wound, which must have been sorer for himself than for the lad ; because surely the handle of that knife was even sharper than its point. And Isaac's soul relinquished uncomplainingly his fresh young life, and all those innocent hopes he had nourished regarding his future. The narrative is fact, but symbol as well as fact. Our spirit is to take our body, and carry it as a free and unmurmuring victim to God in Jesus Christ. The sacrifice originates within, and then spreads to the verge and fringe of our complex nature. First, He Who is our Saviour and Master "runs away to heaven with our heart," as the saint of the Covenant portrayed the conquest in that pictorial language of his; and afterwards, as he said again, we "eat, drink, sleep, journey, speak and think for God"—it is a sheer impossibility to withhold from Him the looks, the senses, the passions, and the energies of the body. You see how spontaneous and how universal the tribute ought to be.

III

Finally, there is a hint here of a treasure which is priceless.

Jeremy Taylor and the moralists are right, when they insist that everything depends on a pure intention and on the motives which only God can read. But the best motives and intentions would be unavailing, unless we had bodily members and faculties with which to give practical effect to them. Our aspirations are fruitless till they are translated into the language of the lips, and the swift ministry of the feet, and the beneficence of hands which do not weary in well-doing. Long before He appeared in our flesh Christ loved us. His delights were with the children of men from an eternal past. But we had not the manifestation and assurance of His love until He took the form of a bond-servant. Then eyes like ours saw the shepherdless sheep, and looked their compassions on the chief of sinners. Then feet like ours hurried the Father's Well-Beloved from place to place in quest of us:

Quærens me sedisti lassus.

Then hands like ours were scarred by the nails, as He hung for our salvation on the Cross. And if Christ needed the body which God had prepared for Him, we cannot dispense with our bodies if, on our more finite scale, we are to glorify the Father and to do good to men. Our looks should be refined into the spirituality and the friendliness of Jesus. Our speech should publish

86

His Gospel in His Own accents, at once so winning, so searching, and so authoritative. Our feet, like His feet, should be literally tired in doing the work of God—an outward exhaustion and fatigue which are tokens of an inward and undecaying joy. If we are well and strong, we can fight for Him and refuse to rest, as British soldiers have been proud to fight in Picardy and Palestine for King George. If we are suffering and sick, we can reveal His presence within us, and can preach His sufficiency, by the strange light on our features and the good courage in our words. In one of her letters Elizabeth Barrett tells Robert Browning of a picture she had seen—" a portrait of Rembrandt by himself which, if his landscapes, as they say, were ' dug out of nature,' looks as if it were dug out of humanity. Such a rugged, dark, deep, subterraneous face, yet inspired ! —seeming to realize that God took clay and breathed into the nostrils of it. There are both the clay and the divinity." Both the clay and the divinity are ours, when God inhabits us ; and the body is a treasure essential and precious.

87

No marvel, therefore, that Clement should hand down the Agraphon, " Keep the flesh pure, and preserve the seal unsullied." No marvel that Paul should *beseech* us, anxiously, yearningly, to *present our bodies a living sacrifice.*

X

THIS IS THE MARKMAN SAFE
AND SURE

A T the saddest moment in David's life the beautiful thing happened. *Ittai answered the king and said, As the Lord liveth, and as my lord the king liveth, surely in what place my lord the king shall be, whether in death or life, even there also will thy servant be* (2 Samuel xv. 21). It was as if, when the night is at its darkest, a star suddenly sent its radiance through the pitchy gloom; or as if, in a lull of the storm, a bird's voice, lark's or thrush's, should be heard singing clear and strong. It was a token of good from God Himself.

I

Ittai is picture and pattern of the highest

character. He might have been the original
of Herbert's " markman safe and sure,"

> Who never melts or thaws
> At close tentations; when the day is done,
> His goodnesse sets not, but in darke can runne.

Or he might have inspired Wordsworth's
Happy Warrior,

> Who comprehends his trust, and to the same
> Keeps faithful with a singleness of aim.

Stranger although he was, and nurtured in
paganism, it moves us to noble issues to
linger in his company.

For he had the soldier's hardihood.
Whether in death or life, whether the sun
was shining or the snow was falling, his mind
was firm. No prosperity the enemy could
offer him would soften the sinews of his soul.
No adversity he might himself be summoned
to endure would daunt the fixity of his
purpose. He had taken his stand; and, let
there be as many devils as tiles on the housetops, he must abide by his post. Not
without significance is it that we have such
inspiriting portraits of soldiers in the Bible
—Joshua, and the centurion at whom Jesus

marvelled, and Cornelius of Cæsarea. Followers of the Prince of Peace as we are, we can never dispense with the soldierly qualities. Decision—for nothing is more abhorrent to Christ than the indifferent neutrality which halts and wavers between God and the world. Straightforwardness—the frankest and manliest espousal of His cause. And courage, which never counts the campaign lost, never acknowledges defeat, and refuses to be overwhelmed by difficulty : " the arms of the Republic," wrote Edward Gibbon, " often repulsed in battle, were always victorious in war." Ittai the soldier calls us to gird on his armour.

And he had the subject's loyalty. *My lord the king*, he said ; and on those leal lips the vow was fine gold without trace or mixture of alloy. What does such loyalty mean for the disciples of Jesus Christ ? It means that we have turned definitively from all fictitious and spurious liberty. There is a necessary and glorious freedom without which we cannot live ; but, side by side with it, there is a counterfeit freedom, anarchic and lawless, which would let our headstrong wills carry us where they liked. This false Florimell, whom "a wicked spright yfraught with fawning guyle" inhabits—this untruth seducing us in the garb of truth—we have abjured absolutely and are for ever done with; for us the "enchanted damzell" has "vanished into nought." It means, further, that we have selected our side and our Leader with our eyes open. We are not blind machines. We are responsible men, and have chosen where we shall be found, maintaining the forgotten truth, defending the unwelcome requirement, allying ourselves with the Christ for Whom numbers have little regard. And it means, as the French General put it, *J'y suis, j'y reste* : that where we stand, we remain. We are not the sport of conflicting winds. We are determined to stay by the flag and by the Captain. He must never have to ask us, *Will ye also go?* —never have to mourn, *Demas hath forsaken Me.* Ittai counsels us to the loyal-heartedness which had rather die than swerve and trim and change.

Moreover, he had the friend's constancy.

It made no difference that the romance and glamour which clung about David's youth had in large measure faded ; nor that his master was a fugitive, maligned by bitter tongues, driven from his palace, and confronted by a future of uncertainty and foreboding. Indeed, these things added fuel to the fires of his attachment, and gave it new elements of chivalry and guardianship. He was a comrade like that Duke George of Freundsberg, who spoke out his goodwill to Luther when Luther was in the thick of his battle at Worms. So must we love Christ, under Whose roof we have dwelt, at Whose table we have sat, by Whose blood we are redeemed. The days of His mourning are not yet ended. From how many quarters He is exiled, His truth contradicted, His redemption scorned, Himself repelled and refused ! There was a Roman Emperor, a weak and unlovable old man, Sulpicius Galba, and in the Forum his litter was attacked by the followers of his rival, and he was done to death. None struck a blow for him except one man, the centurion Sempronius Densus, who warned off the mob with his vine-stick, and drew his sword, and fought a long time till he was cut down from behind. One man, among a million the sun looked on that day, " worthy of the Roman discipline." Our Lord is as different from Galba as summer is from winter. He is " the young Prince of glory," and " from His head, His hands, His feet, sorrow and love flow mingling down." We never saw His like. Surely we shall utter a word for Him, and surely we shall comfort Him by some helpful deed, when, as it were, His back is at the wall. If we fail our Friend of friends then, Ittai of Gath and Sempronius Densus will put us to shame.

And Ittai had the worshipper's reverence. *As the Lord liveth*—it was the sacred and solemn oath he swore. Coming from the idolatries of Philistia, he had witnessed the purer religion of David's court and camp, had hearkened to prayers and psalms which moved his soul, had felt himself breathing a healthier and heavenlier air. Now, at the parting of the ways, at the hour of crisis when a man's innermost mind is declared, he must ring out the conviction which had

been growing strong within him that
Jehovah was a thousand times better than
Dagon. Whether he lived, he would live
henceforward unto the God of Israel;
whether he died, he would die unto Him.
And we—how is it with us? For Christ's
dear sake are we surrendering all the idols,
not in dogmatic profession only, but in
practical and serious fact? Some of them
are unmistakably ugly, like the fish-god of the
Philistines. But others are invested with
indescribable charm, and with a tender and
mighty magnetism of their own. Yet the
most innocent among them, and the most
winning, may not usurp His solitary place.
Not merely from all our filthiness, but from
all our idols—a separation which is harder
to achieve — may God the Holy Spirit
cleanse us! For thus only we shall be of the
family of the old Gittite.

II

For a minute or two, we may bring Ittai
into still closer connection with David's
Son and David's Lord. He did not know

the name of our Saviour ; but, like Ruth of Moab, he comes from a far country to trust and be at home under the shadow of His wings. Of the Syrian courtier Naaman, and the Syrian mother whose name is concealed from us but whose faith Jesus praised, John Calvin says, " It is certain that they were imbued with principles which gave some taste of Christ." Our Philistine saint, we may depend upon it, would have won from the Genevan theologian the same verdict. He, also, is imbued with principles which give some taste of Christ. It may well be—shame on us who make the confession !—that he understands Christ better than we ourselves do.

In what place my Lord the King shall be, even there also shall Thy servant be. And Jesus leaves His throne as David did, though it is His Own exceeding grace which drives Him forth to banishment and poverty. His will be a longer circuit than David's, and it will make Him acquainted with shamefuller depths. Do we reiterate Ittai's *sacramentum,* and plant our foot wherever our Master has left the print of His shoe ? I find Him

at Bethlehem a helpless little Child ; and
do I reject all my vain and fancied wealth,
my pride and righteousness and strength,
as He forsook His supernal and heavenly
treasures ? I find Him in Nazareth, waiting
in quietness until God bids Him be up and
doing ; and do I tarry the Lord's leisure
without a question and without a complaint ?
I see Him during the three years of ministry,
His soul straitened until everything has been
accomplished ; and does His flame of zeal
burn in me ? In Gethsemane I sit watching
about a stone's cast off ; He drinks the cup,
although His humanity quivers and trembles ;
and is this how I submit to the suffering which
God appoints ? I stand beneath the Cross ;
and am I divided from my old life and from
all self-pleasing by a gulf, an abyss, as un-
bridgeable as this death of deaths ? *In what
place, whether in death or life, even there also.*
O, it involves much, and it pierces deep !

But Christ deserves the vow as David
never did, and His trumpets call us to a
holier war than the melancholy duel against
Absalom. And if He had a wider circle to
traverse, and a more swelling Jordan to

cross, He is back again in His kingly palace at Jerusalem, to promise us His Own triumph, and to exchange our weakness for the unflagging and invincible strength of His Own Spirit. Therefore the feeblest among us need not fear to say, *Thine am I, Lord Jesus Christ, and on Thy side, Thou Son of God and Son of Man.*

XI

IN THE MIDST OF THE YEARS

TO the prophet Habakkuk "the problem of problems," Dr. A. B. Davidson has said, "was God." He felt as Job felt, *It is God that maketh my heart faint, and the Almighty that troubleth me.* For his was a brooding, reflecting, questioning soul; and God's thoughts and ways perplexed him. Why did He tolerate the sin of Jerusalem? And, then, why did He swing to the opposite extreme, and punish that sin through the agency of men so tyrannical and brutal as the Chaldeans? These were mysteries hard to reconcile with His holy love. But if Habakkuk's mind was puzzled, his heart pointed constantly to its pole. God was more than the problem of problems; He was the shelter of shelters, and the home of homes. The prophet would wait for

Him, to make the rough places plain in His Own time. Meanwhile, he gave himself to prayer. He asked God to renew His ancient doings and deliverances. At this late hour in His children's history let Him repeat for them the miracles of the Exodus. *O Lord, revive Thy work in the midst of the years ; in the midst of the years make it known* (Habakkuk iii. 2).

It is the best of prayers for you and me.

I

What are some of the elements in the revival which we need ?

A deeper penitence is one. We want and require more consciousness of sin, and more sense of shame and guilt because of sin. " Think," Mr. Cyril Bardsley says, " of a walk with Christ through our streets, of a talk with Christ about the public-houses and the people we meet and the posters we see. Think of Christ having in His hands all the papers from the bookstalls. Think of Him in our churches, and outside our churches in our Christian homes on His

Own day; in our factories and shops; in the luxurious houses of the rich, and in the squalid houses of the poor." We must be brought to view these things through His eyes, until we are utterly humbled because of our slothful acquiescence in them and our cowardly failure to protest against them. We have not been His witnesses, and He has not been able to use us. The first ingredient in revival is sorrow for our silence, our slumber, our pusillanimity, and our sin.

A firmer belief is a second element. In epochs of genuine spiritual awakening neglected truth leaps to the forefront, and is grasped with new intelligence and more questionless decision. Perhaps, as at the Reformation, the truth of the soul's immediate access to God. Or, as in William Carey's day, the truth of Christ's kinghood over the wide world. Or the truth of holiness through simple and continuous faith, which to many in more recent years has been like a revelation from heaven itself. It is a great experience when truth ceases to be something which we take for granted;

when, instead, it becomes something *living and active*, which vibrates through us like a passion, and dominates all our thinking and willing and doing. What if, in our time, one mighty conviction which we must have restirred in our too slack and easy souls is that of the Majesty and Sovereignty of God ? Would it not bring us a reverence, an awe, and a discipline, which we have largely lost, and which it is essential that we should recover ? " O Lord," let us cry, " give us a firmer belief."

A third element in revival is a completer unworldliness. There is no sanctity in asceticism, no superior holiness in withdrawal from the common lot. But the followers of One Whom love led to become poor—

> Our God Who on a tree
> His blood did spill,
> Only to purchase our goodwill—

have assuredly no right to prize their comforts more than they prize perishing men, or to hoard and keep that which they should be laying out for the furtherance of His cause. Long ago, Wiclif's Poor Preachers carried the evangel through

England. Long ago, the Poor Men of Lyons ushered in the spring in southern France and in the Valleys of the Alps. We want to be rebaptized into a similar detachment from earthly gains and goods.

And a braver enthusiasm is yet another element. Our religion is too prosaic. It will not depart from the traditions of the fathers. It is guided by the stereotyped patterns shaped and fixed for it by the majority. Sir George Trevelyan writes a very noble account of a thrilling episode in the Indian Mutiny—the defence for ten long days before relief came, by a mere handful of Europeans and loyal Sikhs, against thousands of rebel Sepoys, of the little house at Arrah. When he has told the splendid story, he goes on, " There are moments when it is good to turn from the perusal of the share list to the contemplation of this spirit, which is prepared to dare all and endure all." It is a spirit which is lacking in too many Christians— the frankness and the fortitude which keep Christ's flag flying in the teeth of the crowd. We are afraid to enter on untried paths, to break away from customary pieties, and to do anything original and difficult for His sake. We should " scorn the consequence," and we should adventure more.

II

Such is the revival we must ask. And why should we desire God's interposition immediately ?

It is because, as Habakkuk says, we are *in the midst of the years*. Far behind the prophet lay the marvels of the Exodus ; the hour had struck for a fresh unveiling of the heavenly glory ; let the Lord illuminate and vitalize the dull and lifeless present. So we may urge Him that, amongst ourselves, it is once more time to reiterate the signs and wonders of the former days, of which our fathers have told us.

In the midst of the years disillusionment creeps over the spirit. When we are young in the family of the Father, we move through a wonderland where things are inexpressibly rare and beautiful. God's righteousness joining with His mercy for our ransom, a Saviour both human and divine, our personal call and our triumphant justification—here is a succession of marvels. "Those pure and virgin apprehensions I had in my infancy," exclaims Thomas Traherne, "and that divine light wherewith I was born, are the best unto this day wherein I can see the universe." But the new birth's virgin apprehensions and fountain light fade as we travel farther from our conversion; and God must reawaken our amazement over His power and grace in Christ Jesus. *In the midst of the years* unbelief comes back to insinuate its doubts. In the soul's day-break how simple, direct, and undisturbed faith is! but the hours and weeks and months run on, and round faith the diffi-culties gather in battalions. When we look at Nature, everything appears material and hastening towards death and dust. When we look at the Bible, it is not so crystal clear as we wish it to be. When we look at Life, its losses and sorrows shake our confidence in the Father. With the man's wider and deeper perceptions God must restore to us the child's unfaltering trust. *In the midst of the years* pride lifts its head again. Newborn into the household, we never imagine that we are sufficient of ourselves; we are a complex of emptinesses and penuries; we have " no language but a cry." But, with the advance of our Christian experience, a feeling of self-congratulation invades our souls. Have we not rendered our service ? and is not the believing society richer for our presence and our help ? But we have nothing which we have not received, and we must kneel and seek afresh the humility and the meekness of our first love. And *in the midst of the* taxing, testing, fatiguing *years* weariness assails the most buoyant heart. It is hard to persevere in succour and intercession, when our ministry seems to work no deliverance in the earth. It is hard to fight for God, when He is Himself invisible. We are tired, and our hands hang down. Must He not lead us anew to the wells of an undecaying youth ? In the face of moral and spiritual needs so patent and so powerful, must He not give the Church and the Christian what Mr.

J. H. Oldham calls " a more passionate, exultant, venturesome faith in the Gospel " and " in its right to rule the whole life of the world " ?

III

Yes, and He will; if we but fulfil our part. And what is that ?

Across the sea, on one of the walls of the Public Library in Boston, is a marvellous mural painting by Mr. Sargent. Twelve Jews, representatives of the Twelve Tribes, are huddled in the foreground, a naked and despondent group. Above them stand their oppressors. To the left is Pharaoh, exquisite, effeminate, deadly cruel. He lifts the scourge in one hand, and with the other he grips the hair of the captives. On the right is the Assyrian king, duller, heavier, with knotted limbs. He presses down the yoke on the prisoners, and draws back his sword for a merciless blow. But one of the Jews rises to implore the help of God, and the hands of the rest are raised in supplication. And Jehovah hears the cry. The cherubim fly before Him, their wings a glowing crimson. They hide His face. But from behind the wings come His everlasting arms. The slender Pharaoh He represses with a touch. The brute tyranny of the Assyrian He holds in a grasp of tremendous power. That is our hope. Behind the crimson wings are the strong Arms, and the Heart which is unspeakably tender.

But we must cry, as the Jews cried from their slavery. We must pray for revival, as Habakkuk prayed, earnestly, longingly, continuously. This is our part, the part of the violent who take the Kingdom by force, the part of the lowly who knock and knock until the Father's door is opened wide. " The sea is out, and I cannot bring a wind and cause it to flow again ; only I wait on the shore till the Lord sends a full sea." So Samuel Rutherfurd wrote from his prison in Aberdeen. They who wait on the shore till the Lord sends a full sea are not disappointed.

> Far back, through creeks and inlets making,
> Comes silent, flooding in, the main

XII

TAKE TIME TO BE HOLY

IN his vision of a Temple of God, more sublime than any to which the Twelve Tribes went up, Ezekiel saw many priests busying themselves in ministry. And it seemed to him that a divine Voice enjoined these priests, before they left the sanctuary, to change their vestments of glory and beauty for a less sacred dress, in which they might mingle with the crowd. *Then shall they not go out of the Holy Place into the outer court, but there they shall lay their garments wherein they minister, for they are holy ; and they shall put on other garments, and shall approach to that which pertaineth to the people* (Ezekiel xlii. 14). This ordinance of the Lord has its teaching for us in our day.

I

It speaks of the worship which takes pains.
You watch those servants as they go up
and down God's strange and unearthly
house. They have clothed themselves in
robes of the costliest and fairest linen. They
will be for a good while in the King's chamber,
and they are at no little trouble to prepare
beforehand. Their ministry necessitates
something of previous arrangement and
personal carefulness. It is a complete withdrawal from the outside world. It is an ex-
penditure not of one hour but of a succession
of hours. It involves the laying aside of their
customary raiment, and the putting on of
new raiment which more befits the presence
of the Most High God.

Is there anything like this, I wonder, in
our life of worship? In Highland glens,
and in the sea-drenched islands round our
coasts, the visitor comes on rude and simple
churches, to the building of which a world
of toil and affection and faith and pains has
gone. Men carted the sand and the wood
from distant places. Women and children

carried the stones in their own hands from the shore. They never grudged the labour, the weariness, and the sacrifice. Would that you and I resembled them more than we do ! Is it easy to pray in secret ? We must abjure every distraction. We must consider what we need to ask. We must invoke the Holy Spirit's aid. We must survey the greatness, the holiness, the truth, and the grace of God, to Whom we come. A friend, Principal D. M. M'Intyre, sends me a privately printed address on Andrew Alexander Bonar. He dwells especially on the vigilance with which Dr. Bonar mastered the science and the art of prayer. "He used to realize that the constant effort of the evil one was to turn him aside from prayer ; consequently he watched his performance of the duty with great exactness, testing scrupulously the reality and intimacy of his intercourse with God. He often found that, when he was engaged in this high exercise, he had to win his way to *access* by conflict with temptations subtle and persistent ; but he persevered till victory was given." Is it easy to search the Word ? It demands concentration. It demands the honest dealing which applies the message to our own lives : "Pray God," one of the wisest of spiritual directors told a correspondent, "to copy His Bible into your conscience, and to write a new book of His doctrine in your heart." And it demands the adoring spirit which never forgets how the Heavenly Lord lives and moves in the rooms and corridors of Holy Scripture. Is it easy to meditate patiently and profitably on the eternal realities ? You must bid good-bye to the clamour of duties, the intrusion of pleasures, the worry of cares. You must set your face steadfastly towards Mount Zion. You must study its laws, its obligations, its excellences, its joys. "If thou canst get but thither," you must say to your soul, "there grows the Flower of Peace " ; but the getting thither signifies intention, recollection, renunciation, adjustment, devotion. It is not to be done without determination.

God grant us grace to pass, every day, into the innermost Temple ! God help us, every day, to strip off the earthly garments, and to robe ourselves in the holy dress !

II

Further, the command speaks of the soul which has its own secret.

When their service behind the curtains and before the altars was over, the priests whom Ezekiel saw divested themselves of their sanctuary raiment. God kept something to Himself, something known only to His ministers and to Him. He would not permit thoughtless and unworthy eyes to scrutinize a garb which was so unusual, so resplendent, and so stately. Before they quitted the chamber where they met with Him, His representatives must resume their ordinary clothing. They were not allowed to lay bare their deepest experience ; part of it, at least, was hidden from the curiosity of the multitude.

Now, Christ expects His disciples to declare frankly the great things He has done and is doing for them. He

> doth with us as we with torches do,
> Not light them for themselves ; for if our virtues
> Did not go forth of us, 'twere all alike
> As if we had them not. Spirits are not finely touch'd
> But to fine issues,—

to fine issues, and lowly acknowledgments, and eager ministries, and unqualified consecrations. In other parts of Scripture we read that the priests in the Temple were anointed with sweet spices, whose perfume accompanied them wherever they went; and the genuine Christian has poured on him an ointment which should bewray itself everywhere and always. But there are things not to be published on the housetops. The grace we have received holds heights in it we cannot scale and depths we cannot plumb. An American poet portrays a child on Calvary :

> The Cross is tall,
> And I too small
> To reach His hand
>   Or touch His feet;
> But on the sand
>   His footprints I have found,
> And it is sweet
>   To kiss the holy ground.

That is often the utmost we can do—to kiss the holy ground, in silence, in faith, and in an unutterable ecstasy of love. Moreover, we ought not to disclose everything. To unveil the most hallowed passages of

our salvation, its keenest griefs and its
richest joys, is to inflict positive injury on
ourselves. It lessens humility. It rubs off
some of the delicate bloom from the fruit
of the Spirit. It makes the Most Holy
Place of the soul a trodden and public highway. And it is not calculated to win others.
They do not understand this intimacy of
communion, this exquisite pain, this third
heaven of rapture and emotion. It is a
more rudimentary Gospel which we should
impart to them. It is the porch and not the
penetralia of the Temple with which, in the
first instance, they must make acquaintance.

Thus he who is the Lord's priest puts off
his turban and tunic ere he returns to the
outer court. He keeps to himself his incommunicable secret. And do we? Is
there a mystery we may not unfold? Is
there a song of songs which the deep heart
sings, but which can never be set to words?
Is there a Lord enshrined within, Who talks
with us alone, as He talked with Nicodemus
in the *aliyah* by night, with Mary Magdalene
in the garden of the resurrection, with John
when he was in the Isle and in the Spirit?

III

One thing more. The command speaks of the God Who is never far away.

The very instruction to lay past the holy dress reminds the priests that, although they have left the shrine, God abides in it still and will be ready for them whensoever they come back. They have only to retrace their steps and to clothe themselves afresh in their snowy robes, and once more He will lift up His countenance on them and give them peace. " I have found the Lord easy to be entreated," Thomas Boston testifies, " and recovery to be gained without long onwaiting." It is a witness to which many of us can add our Amen.

The raiment of the soul's dedication may not, perhaps, be resumed so quickly and with such facility as the priest's tiara and stole. The solemn truth is that it is a serious error and a real disloyalty ever to throw it aside. If we cannot always be employed in specific acts of worship, and if the Transfiguration Mount must be left for the labours and sacrifices and temptations that are waiting below, we are guilty of sin whenever we forfeit the worshipful temper and the transfigured life. Yet God is He Who heals our backsliding. The engrossments of business may have been our snare. Then let us confess that our work has held us too exclusively, dulling our ears to the everlasting chime. He will forgive. He will teach us to carry a detached and heaven-possessed heart into the necessary routine. And He will make Himself so essential that, with every striking of the clock, our spirits will pause to talk deliberately with Him and to reap the golden harvests of such fellowship. Or the wintrinesses of sorrow may have been clouding His goodness and mercy. " I would say," Dr. John Ker wrote to a friend, " that it is not when our afflictions are heavy and fresh that we derive much benefit from them. We are stunned. We feel little else than the blow. It is *afterwards* that they yield the peaceable fruits of righteousness." We know this blessed Afterwards, when we are shut in with God, and He shows us that our trials are part of the peculiar and distinctive favour which He bears to His Own. Or the pitiable weaknesses of moral failure and spiritual declension have sundered us from the happiness we had when His candle shined on our heads. That is unpardonable. It is thrice and four times heinous and without excuse in His Blood-bought and Spirit-quickened children, for whom in Christ Jesus He has provided a continual victory. But we confess the shameful infidelity, and He cleanses us from its stain and frees us from its power. He makes and keeps us constant, loving, clingingly and persistently trustful. Again He changes the filthy garments of our disobedience, and the rough sackcloth of our penitence, into the gleaming attire of His ministering priest.

Let us get back to the sanctuary, and the God of the sanctuary will revisit us in the marvel of His enduring kindness. For He giveth liberally and upbraideth not.

XIII

WE FAINT NOT

BUT many a time, in our own experience as sworn disciples of the Lord Jesus Christ, the temptation comes to us to faint. Perhaps it is the vision of self—never a consoling and uplifting vision to the sons and daughters of God. Perhaps it is the pressure of difficulty; outside, as well as inside, there are a thousand things to damp and dismay. Perhaps it is the flight of time; *that* smothers and kills a host of high resolves, of thankful thoughts, of inspiriting ideals. And thus we faint.

Yes; but let us bless God that His remedies to check and heal and banish the fainting are always near and always sufficient.

I

We meet the vision of self by the calling in of Grace. *As we have received mercy,*

says St. Paul, *we faint not* (2 Corinthians
iv. 1).

When did we receive mercy ? When we
were as bad as we could be. When we were
not dying but dead in trespasses and sins.
When we could not utter a syllable in our
own defence, or move a finger for our own
recovery and release. Nobody except God
in Jesus Christ would have compassionated
us. No other would, or could, have devised
and performed the tremendous task of redeeming those who were sunk so low. But
He did it. He was not deterred by our black
undeservingness. Let it be that, in ourselves, we continue capable of all failure, all
perversity, and all evil. We examine our
souls ; and we are confronted by disabilities
which seem ineradicable, doubts which are
ever suggesting their scepticisms and nega-
tions, promptings to many unworthy com-
promises with a world that is totally antag-
onistic to Christ, indolence and cowardice
and procrastination and pride, motives and
desires and tempers and purposes and
pictures which are anything but heavenly.
O, the spectacle is humbling enough. It

will be fatal to let the examination become over-sedulous, over-scrupulous, over-morbid; nothing but despair lies along that path. We must counterbalance and correct the vision of self by the vision of the Love which self at its worst was not able to affright and drive away. God's mercy did not speak its final word, when it forgave us at first through the shedding of Christ's precious blood. To this instant it remains available, efficacious, and free. It is prepared to take charge of our daily progress and perfecting, as well as of our initial righteousness. Do not let us fix our gaze so perseveringly on our demerit that we have no eyes to behold the medicine our Lord has provided for just such pithless and strengthless souls. Once it was the medicine of the atoning Cross; now it is that of the longsuffering and prevailing Spirit; and it would be hard to determine which of these two is the more invulnerable. Men and women who have received mercy ought never to faint again. Against all disquietudes they should call in the Grace that is omnipotent, summoning the great new world of Heaven to redress the disordered balance in the old world of their hearts and lives.

II

We meet the pressure of difficulty by the falling back upon God. *Men ought always to pray*—it is the Master Who speaks now, and not the Apostle—*always to pray, and not to faint* (Luke xviii. 1).

" When obstacles and trials seem like prison-walls to be "; when literature is often hostile and poisonous, and science discovers no trace of the living Lord in the works of His hands; when society has its laugh and its pity for the people whose treasures are behind the veil; when the very Church is cold and unsympathetic; and when Satan and his angels are raining down their fiery darts on " the little flock named after Christ's Own heart "—then is the time to make much of God, to throw ourselves into His Everlasting Arms, and to link our powerlessness with His infinite and unchangeable powers. Dr. De Witt of Princeton writes impressively of Jonathan Edwards and his " immediate perception of the spiritual universe as the reality of realities." God, he says, became vivid to Augustine through the mediation of Augustine's experience of sin. He drew near to Dante through Dante's love of Beatrice. He taught Calvin His absolute and universal sovereignty through Calvin's revolt from the sovereignty of the human head of an earthly Church. But He spoke to Edwards mouth to mouth and face to face. "Except the apostle called by eminence 'the Theologian,' St. John the Divine, I know no other great character in history," Dr. De Witt asserts, " of whom it can so emphatically be said that, when he ' breathed the pure serene ' of the spiritual world, he did so as native and to the manner born." You remember that, when Edwards read these words of Scripture, *Now unto the King eternal, immortal, invisible, the only wise God, be honour and glory, for ever,* he was suddenly moved with a sort of inward delight in God and celestial things. You recollect that, even when others were round about him, he often seemed to himself to be alone in the mountains or in some solitary wilderness, conversing familiarly with Christ, and wrapt and swallowed up in God. If we but

123

practised the Presence with some little degree of Jonathan Edwards's sureness and immediacy, our hands would not hang down any more, or our knees be feeble. And how shall we acquire the habit, and possess ourselves of the talisman ? How, but by prayer. By getting alone into our chamber, with the door shut, and there pouring out our souls before Him, and lingering in His company till we are aware of no one but Himself—not of the enemies, but of Himself, King of kings and Lord of lords, glorious in holiness, fearful in praises, doing wonders, Whose name shall endure as long as the sun, Whose servants and friends can never anywhere or anyhow be put to shame. We shall rise from our knees to sing the Reformation battle-hymn :

> And were this world all devils o'er,
> And watching to devour us,
> We lay it not to heart so sore ;
> Not they can overpower us.

We shall come down from our Mount like Moses from his, with our faces shining and the fearsome shadows chased from very nook and cranny of our souls. When we fall back upon God, we do not dream of fainting. In darkest shades, when God appears, our dawning is begun.

III

And we meet the flight of time by the looking away unto Jesus. *Consider Him that endured such contradiction of sinners*, the writer to the Hebrews says, *that ye faint not* (Hebrews xii. 3).

Time is against the Christian. Time can chill. When his salvation was new, what a horror he felt at sin! what a fire for Christ burned in his every nerve and fibre! what vows his will registered! what a tender, delicate, ardent, vehement kindness was the kindness of his youth! But the weeks, the months, the years have stolen imperceptibly and ceaselessly on; and airs and depressions and fatigues of the prison-house have begun to insinuate themselves into the heart which exulted then, and meant to exult to the last, in the marvel of its freedom and the exceeding grace of its Lord. But here is what neutralizes and defeats the dulling influence of time, so that it shall wield over us no soporific and paralyzing bewitchment: to consider, and to be ever considering afresh, the Jesus Who

climbed the Hill of Reproach for us, and Who
nailed Himself for our sakes to the accursed
Tree. That will do three things. First, it
will make us ashamed of the notion of revert-
ing to the ease and indifference of the life
we have left, or of faltering because of the
hardships of the life to which we have been
called ; what, we shall ask ourselves, is our
severest suffering compared with the sorrow,
the desolation, and the death which our
Ransomer bore ? And then it will re-establish
our love for Him Who first loved us and so
loved us ; deny Him, return to anything He
disapproves, refuse anything which He appoints and gives !—we shall recoil from it as
a sheer and hateful impossibility. And, lest
these should not be enough, it will constrain
us to receive more and more continuously the
light and life of the Holy Ghost, Who reveals
this Jesus, Who magnifies Him, Who binds
us to Him by cords which nothing will relax
and destroy. We do not, we dare not, we
cannot, faint when it is our constant custom,
our refuge " at morning-break and through
the live-long day," to look away unto Jesus
Christ.

XIV

A DEEP BUT DAZZLING
DARKNESS

THE phrase, you remember, is Henry
Vaughan's :

> There is in God—some say—
> A deep but dazzling darkness ; as men here
> Say it is late and dusky, because they
> See not all clear.

So Hannah felt, when she sang, *There is
none holy as the Lord* (1 Samuel ii. 2). And
so, many centuries afterwards, Mary felt
too, when this was her adoring word, *Holy
is His Name* (Luke i. 49). For it is God's
holiness which makes Him " dark with
excessive bright."

I

In a double aspect the holiness is presented to us. It is an unflecked diamond,

127

white from soil and spot; and it is a passionate ruby, warm and aflame. It is the uttermost of recoil from sin; and it is the uttermost of attachment for good.

Holy is His Name. That is, He stands at the opposite pole from our evil. He is untouched by the festering leprosy which has crept and eaten like a cancer through the warp and woof, the surfaces and the secrets, of our nature. The contrast is complete between God and everything false, or selfish, or wicked. How should this recollection affect us? Surely it should bring rebuke, and confusion, and the knowledge of imminent danger, and the prospect of unescapeable condemnation, if we are still wedded to our transgression. The "militant purity" of God, a recent theologian has written, is "a mighty thing to believe in, but a tremendous thing to live with"; it is nothing short of His sentence of death decreed against our sin. But, as truly, it is an infinitely hope-enkindling and heartening thing. If we hate our evil and are earnest to have it destroyed, the memory of His sovereign holiness ought to beget unfailing expectation and cheer, because it pronounces and it seals the doom of whatever in us is opposed to His Own stainlessness. For our souls the roseate promise of the ancient prophet will be performed, *Egypt shall be a desolation, and Edom a desolate wilderness; but Judah shall dwell for ever, and Jerusalem from generation to generation.*

But God's holiness is the red heat of the ruby, as well as the flashing crystal of the diamond. It is the greatest of positives, as certainly as it is the greatest of negatives. If He is the contradiction of spiritual ugliness, He is the embodiment of spiritual grace and perfection. "And what," cried Augustine, "is all that any man can say when speaking of Thee, my God, my Life, my Joy?" "Even the most eloquent are dumb," he confessed. They have need of "one word more." They will require to call to their aid a language hitherto unminted, "fit, and fair, and simple, and sufficient." Yet Augustine essayed the impossibility. "Who is God save our God? Most merciful, yet most just; most hidden, yet most near ; most beautiful, yet most strong ; stable, yet incomprehensible ; never young, and never old ; ever in action, yet ever at rest ; still gathering, yet lacking nothing; supporting, filling, and overshadowing all things. Thou art jealous, without uneasiness ; repentest, yet grievest not ; art angry, yet always calm ; changest Thy works, while Thy purpose is unchanged ; recoverest what Thou findest, yet didst never lose ; art never in need, and yet art gladdened by gains." It is a soaring and satisfying portraiture; but the august, entrancing, awful Original is ten thousand times more astonishing, more soaring, and more satisfying. May we hunger to know and resemble Him, so far as it is permitted man to know and to resemble ! May we be smitten into Augustine's worshipfulness and love—" Say unto my soul, *I am thy salvation.* Say it so that I may hear. I will run after this voice, and take hold on Thee. O, hide not Thou Thy face from me ! *Moriar ne moriar, ut eam videam.* Let me die seeing it—only let me see Thy face." No voice has such music in it. No face shines with such wonderful light. Death would be a small price to pay for one hearing of the music and a moment's beholding of the light. But to hear and to behold God is not death; it is the *life which is life indeed*.

II

The holiness of God has its high and difficult problems to solve.

The problem of sin, for example. Sin is the antithesis of His character and government, the flouting of His law, the sore disappointment of His heart. When holiness confronts sin, there will be the flame of hot indignation, and the sword of shattering judgment. But grief will mingle with the indignation and the judgment, an unfathomable grief for the sinner whom sin befools. And in so dread a contest between such irreconcilable forces, the victory must lie with holiness. That which is not Godlike cannot prevail in God's world, and sin marches slowly but certainly to condign defeat. "There was an Ocean of Darkness and Death," George Fox said once;

" but an Ocean of Light and Love flowed over the Ocean of Darkness and Death."

Then there is the problem of salvation. If none is holy as the Lord, how can He take to His embrace those who have gone voluntarily into the far country, and have chosen to besmirch themselves with the mire and clay ? Human philosophy has no answer to the baffling query ; but God has found the answer. We read it in the self-abnegation of Bethlehem and in the sacrifice of Calvary, in this Cross and sacrifice most of all. God's dear Son, Who, at the Father's bidding and the imperative bidding of His Own heart of exceeding grace, fulfils all righteousness in our room, and dies beneath our curse and for our redemption—He is the Answer. To as many as receive Christ, God is both Just and Justifier, the God of holiness and the God of peace. He will not exact my penalty twice over, " once at my bleeding Surety's hand, and once again at mine." The inhabitants of Domremy went free from their taxes and dues for the Maid's sake who delivered France ; and I go free from my intolerable debts and weighty burdens and crimson iniquities for the Good Shepherd's sake, Who laid down His life for me. Nor is God's holiness tarnished in freeing me; it is magnified and made honourable.

Side by side with the problems of sin and salvation is the problem of love. Can the holiness which brooks no slightest flaw or minutest abatement live within the same God in happy concord and consent with the love which has neither breadth nor length nor depth nor height? Can Hannah and Mary give a true report, *Holy is His Name*, and yet John give a true report, *God is Love*? Yes, both reports are true. Holiness and love are different ingredients in His perfectness; and they have different effects on us, the one chastening us into awe, the other conquering us by the mighty magic of its kindness. But there is no need to persuade them to join hands, as if they had quarrelled; no need even to discuss which is the more fundamental and supreme. They are in closest agreement. Both are indispensable, and both are regnant. The holiness is loving, and the love is holy. The one is eager and resolute to rid us of sin, the other eager and resolute to diadem us with blessing; and the two things are the same thing. Where sin is, blessing cannot be. Where sin is expelled, blessing enters, and thrives, and abounds. The holiness of God and His love move towards one goal and finish one work.

III

God's holiness addresses its demand to us.

There is none holy as the Lord—not the ripest saint, or the most Christlike soul, or the pilgrim who is but a single step removed from the gate and street of the Celestial City. In heaven itself His holiness will continue to be distinguished from ours. We shall be sinless, and the last vestige of our corruptions will have fled—O emancipation most strange and sweet ! But to the perfection of our God there will attach still an independence, an unassailableness, and a solitary radiancy and effulgence

of glory, which must for ever put it on
another plane from yours and mine. That,
however, is not our concern meanwhile.
Here and now we are called to be imitators
of God as dear children. His holiness is
to be a perpetual invitation, an impelling
stimulus, and an imperious pattern.

> We needs must love the highest when we see it,
> Not Lancelot, not another,

the Queen says in the poem, when, after the
madness of her disloyalty, her soul awakes to
perceive Arthur for what he really is. And
we needs must love the Highest when we
see Him. It is forbidden us, it is treason
in a Christian man or woman, to stop short
of our Father's holiness, reflected and re-
produced in ourselves.

The demand would be our despair, if we
were left to our own resources. But we are
not left. Christ our Saviour liberates us
from the guilt and disability of the past, and
the indwelling Spirit supplies our every want
in the present. The Lamb and the Dove
bring the holiness of God to our thresholds,
and communicate it to our very hearts. He

who makes most of the Lamb and the Dove ;
he who, conscious of his weakness, perpetually repairs to the Strength which is supernatural and divine : he catches most of
God, and carries Him consistently and con-
tagiously up and down the world. And so,
as we began with Henry Vaughan, I think
we had best close by falling on our knees
to pray in fellowship with the wise and
devout Silurian :

> There is in God—some say—
> A deep but dazzling darkness ;

and

> O for that Night ! where I in Him
> Might live invisible and dim !

XV

THIS HONOUR HAVE ALL HIS SAINTS

THERE have been times in history when the word Priest inspired alarm and distrust rather than quietness and hope. The priest was dowered with awful dignities and sanctities. He stood between God and the soul of man; and the soul waited on him cowering, trembling, helpless. It knew that, apart from his intervention, it was doomed to bleak despair and irretrievable death. But when St. John penned his hymn of praise to Christ as God, *He made us to be priests unto His Father* (Revelation i. 6), he certainly did not use the word with any sinister meaning. To his mind the priest was not a figure of dread, but a figure of amazing attraction and appeal. He was not the member of a separate and

exclusive caste; the purple robes of the
king are yours and mine and everybody's
when we participate in the salvation of
our Lord, and so are the white robes of
the accepted and prevailing priest. The
barriers are down. The ordination and the
endowment, the responsibility and the
glory, are for each believing soul.

I

*He made us to be priests unto His God and
Father.* So, then, we are in living union
with the High Priest, the Lord Jesus Christ.

In the Old Testament the priest was an
august and imposing personality. There,
in the pre-Christian age, and in the services
of the Jewish tabernacle and temple, he
received the offerings of the people; he
presented their sacrifices to Jehovah; he
lifted up hands of entreaty to plead for
their well-being, and hands of benediction which conveyed to them the goodwill of God. Why has his sacrificing and
mediating ministry lost its validity in the
day of the Gospel? It is because Christ

is enough. He is All we want. We have
one solitary High Priest, Whose fullness
can never be enhanced, and Who in the
nature of things is without partner or rival.
Once for all, He offered His true body and
reasonable soul for our sins on the bleeding
and burning altar of the Cross. In that
offering there is "grace enough for thousands
of new worlds as great as this." And, since
His hour of glorious infamy, He has been
alive for evermore, our Eternal Intercessor
in the heavenly places and at the right hand
of the Majesty on high. It is vain to dream
of adding to the virtue of Calvary, and vain
to imagine that the advocacy of our Paraclete
before the Throne requires to be eked out
by the pleadings of priestly suppliants on
earth. There is an unsurpassable adequacy
about Jesus Christ the Righteous. He is like
the Prince's shield in Spenser's poem—" One
Diamond, perfect, pure, and clean." We cannot improve His lustrous brightness or His
inflexible quality. And when He captures
and keeps our faith and love, His priesthood,
in its meritoriousness and its power, is our
salvation, our shelter, and our security.

We know that He was delivered for our offences. We know that He is raised again for our justification. We find an illimitable worth in His one sacrifice of Himself on the Hill of Reproach. We find an endless potency in His constant presentation of Himself in the Holy of Holies within the veil. Priesthood of our own we do have ; but it is wholly subordinate to Christ's and altogether derived from Christ's. We are " true Aarons," simply because we sing the lowly song :

> Christ is my onely Head,
> My alone onely Heart and Breast,
> My onely Musick, striking me ev'n dead,
> That to the old man I may rest,
> And be in Him new drest.

> So holy in my Head,
> Perfect and light in my deare Breast,
> My doctrine tun'd by Christ—Who is not dead,
> But lives in me while I do rest—
> Come, people ; Aaron's drest.

II

We listen again to John's doxology. *He made us priests unto His God and Father.*

So, then, we belong to the greatest and best fellowship on earth.

Bishop Lightfoot has a classical essay, in which these sentences occur : " The Kingdom of Christ is not limited by the restrictions which fetter other societies, political or religious. It is free, comprehensive, universal. It accepts all comers who seek admission, irrespective of race or caste or sex. It has no sacerdotal system. It interposes no sacrificial tribe between God and man, by whose intervention God is reconciled and man is forgiven. Each individual member holds personal communion with the divine Head. From his Lord directly each obtains pardon, draws strength, and receives grace." What a charter of enfranchisement is here ! What a large room and spacious air ! How unconstrained the invitation, and how fructifying the intercourse ! The door could not be opened more widely. The boon is unobstructed by provisos or enactments, taxes or dues. The Lord stands, with both of His arms extended, to greet and welcome every one who seeks His face. Is it " to

God we speed so fast " ?   Is it the Supreme Intimacy, and nothing less, which will appease us ?   Then we may have God— Father, Redeemer, Holy Ghost—with the shoreless and heart-filling satisfaction He confers, by going to Him for ourselves, without tarrying for churchly sanctions, without setting in motion an elaborate machinery, without leaning on human inter- mediaries and helpers. This, indeed, is the greatest and best fellowship.

It has been said that Christianity, in the idea of its Founder, is " a priestless religion." Priestless it is beyond all controversy and debate, in the sense that it lends no coun- tenance to the pretensions and pomps of those who should have brought God to man and man to God, but who in hundreds of instances forgot their vocation and left it undone. We are not dependent on them. We do not halt and shiver in the outer pre- cincts, whilst they pass in for us to the central shrine. But, in another sense, Christianity is a priest-haunted and priest-crowded religion. For all of us, young and old, rich and poor, white and black, the happycircumstanced and the sorrow-laden, may practise the continual priesthood. Whenever we choose, we can enter the Very Presence of Christ's Father and our Father. We can ask and have His grace and mercy and peace, His succour for ourselves and those we call our friends, His revival for the Church, His redemption for the world. Writing to Alfred Tennyson in 1860, when the *Idylls of the King* had newly appeared, John Ruskin said this : "I think I have seen faces, and heard voices by road and street side, which claimed or conferred as much as ever the loveliest or saddest of Camelot. As I watch them, the feeling continually weighs upon me, day by day, more and more, that not the grief of the world but the loss of it is the wonder of it. I see creatures so full of all power and beauty, with none to understand or teach or save them. The making in them of miracles, and all cast away ; for ever lost as far as we can trace. And no In Memoriam." To transcribe these unknown souls, Ruskin told Tennyson, is " the true task of the modern poet." Then Christ is the Supremest of poets. He is always transcribing the unknown souls, always calling into play the latent power and the undeveloped beauty, always anointing the common people as priests of God's Temple. Enrolment in the proudest empire on earth does not equal these honours and joys.

III

We may think again. *He made us priests unto His God and Father.* So, then, always and in all surroundings, we can be ministrants in the shrine.

What need to look for some ancient and historic sanctuary, or for dedicated hands, or for the fortunate few who have been hallowed by chrism and unction ? " The close, the milkhouse, the stable, the barn," to quote John Bunyan's inventory, will do excellently ; and so will the muddy trenches beside the Somme and the Ancre, and the monotonous sands of Egypt and Mesopotamia, and the decks of battle-cruisers tossing restlessly in the waters of the North Sea. Christ attaches literally no value to trappings and shows, the grandiose and the spectacular. He covets what is spiritual—the love of the heart, the illumination of the mind, the resurrection of the conscience, the obedience of the will. Wherever He encounters these, the ground is holy. In whomsoever He meets them, their possessor is His authentic and anointed priest. Delineating the Church of the Early Centuries, Principal Lindsay narrates how its officebearers, while they might be clergymen in virtue of their call and election to the ministry, nevertheless worked at trades, and carried on mercantile pursuits, and were not separated from their neighbours in ordinary life. The bishop might be a weaver, or a lawyer, or a shepherd, or a shipbuilder. Away in Cilicia, where he was born who was at once apostle and tentmaker, is a graveyard; and on its stones one may read now of a potter and now of a goldsmith, both of whom were presbyters or priests of the local congregation. When the potter shaped his vessel deftly and lovingly on the wheel, when the goldsmith bent above his crucible, when through noonday heat and midnight frost the shepherd shared the experiences of his sheep and lambs, when the weaver kept diligent watch over the threads and shuttles of his loom, they were as sacrosanct as when, on the Lord's Day and in the Lord's House, they presided at the sacrament of the Lord's Supper. It is not outward rite and pageant which God demands. It is the work of faith, the speech of prayer, the labour of love, and the patience of hope. Because all of us in whom His Spirit resides can render Him these, we are all His priests. And because we can render them at any spot and in any hour, we are His priests everywhere and always.

We have obtained Sparta for our heritage, and let us continually adorn Sparta.

XVI

WHERE FEAR ABOUNDS GRACE SUPERABOUNDS

WHO of us does not love that great commandment of our Lord, with its unanswerable reason annexed—*Fear not, little flock ; for it is your Father's good pleasure to give you the kingdom* (Luke xii. 32) ? It is a word on which to base an unfaltering faith, an amaranthine hope, and a full assurance.

I

There is the fear that springs from the knowledge of ourselves ; but Christ vanquishes it by reminding us of the freeness of grace.

Kingdoms have been won by military genius, as Bonaparte fought his way to

147

dominance over France. They have rewarded wise statecraft, as Pericles rose to supremacy in Athens—Pericles, whose one recreation was philosophy, and who was seldom seen except on the road between his house and the popular assembly. Now and then, they have gone to the practical mystic and the soldier saint, as for a few golden weeks Savonarola held the reins of power in Florence. But along none of these paths can we travel to the kingdom of which Jesus spoke. We are altogether unworthy of it. When the veils and excuses fall off, and the revealing Word and the convicting Spirit paint us to our consciences in our true colours, we despair of crossing its threshold. Ours is the hopeless cry, " Such honours and such purities are not for me ! "

But He banishes the inevitable and most proper dread. His verb is not " Strive," nor " Merit," nor " Attain." It is no verb depicting a title which we must assert or an equivalent which we may bring. The very reverse is the case. It depicts God's activity and not our ; and it sets the divine activity before us in its unfettered spontaneousness and undeserved mercy. It is the verb *Give*. God gives the kingdom; not one of us acquires it. An old chronicler, speaking of the Provinces of Lower Austria in 1546, writes that in them "are five sorts of persons— Clergy, Barons, Nobles, Burghers, and Peasants. Of these last," he goes on, "no account is made, because they have no voice in the Diet." But the Peasants, "these last," are really the only people who have a voice in God's Diet. Conscious and confessed nothingness is the irrefragable argument which wins the day at His bar. He bestows His empire on men who have beggared and destroyed themselves. For the sake of One with Whom He is well-pleased, they can have, without money and without price, simply by trusting and taking, all that the King and the kingdom mean—the forgiven heart, the cleansed and renovated character, the fruitful life, the sure and certain hope of immortality. We do not earn; we receive. We do not plan and strain and contend to the uttermost; we put our hand in Jesus Christ's hand, and He leads us in. *Fear not*, our Lord says, *for God gives*.

II

There is the fear that comes from the vision of the inheritance; but Christ nullifies it by reminding us of the purposefulness of grace.

No kingdom is so superlative and so indefectible as this. The glory that was Greece and the grandeur that was Rome look tawdry and common beside it. It is the Gospel, with its blessings in the present and its promises for the future. It is the soul pardoned, purged from old defilements, living in near fellowship with God, tuned to a hundred sacred uses. It is the new heaven and new earth within us now, and the new heaven and new earth around us by and by. But the unapproached uniqueness of it—its magnitude, its fineness and fullness, its unearthly sanctity—appears to put it far beyond our reach. Not only are we ourselves unfit; the realm to which we aspire is too majestical. Imagine a poor man awaking some morning, to be told that the dominion of the Victorias and Edwards and Georges was his—" this precious stone

set in the silver sea," and all the nation-
alities that are linked with it, the Canadas,
the Australias, the Indias, the South Africas.
That Time, and the ocean, and some foster-
ing star, first built up this " kingdom in
kingdom," this " sway in oversway," and
then lavished the whole of it on him, in
order that he might

> stretch one hand to Huron's bearded pines,
> And one on Kashmir's snowy shoulder lay—

what an unbelievable whimsy it would
seem ! Yet that is nothing to the thought
of our inheritance.

And the thought is no unbelievable
whimsy. It is unshakable fact. It is surer
than seedtime and harvest, and day and
night, and sun and moon. Our participa-
tion in the kingdom, Christ declares, depends
on the *good pleasure* of God. The phrase
is memorable and melodious. It affirms
that both God's will and God's heart are
engaged in saving us. He has determined
to do it, and He is joyfully glad to do it.
So He chose us before time began, and He
calls us in the opportune season and crisis
of time, and He garrisons and keeps us until

time shall merge in eternity. He ordains the sorrows which restore and soften our souls, and the disappointments which hold us leaning on Himself, and the delays which increase our desires after the things the eye has not seen. From start to finish it is His doing, and from start to finish it is His delight. God's *good pleasure* gives us the kingdom, in its early blade and ripening ear and full corn, its sunrise and its advancing warmth and its meridian noon. The riches are unsearchable; but the purposefulness of grace makes them our own.

III

There is the fear that arises from the contemplation of God Himself, but Christ stills and hushes it by reminding us of the tenderness of grace.

To whom does the kingdom pertain? To a judge? Beyond question; to the most searching Judge, Who demands truth in the inward parts. To a monarch? Doubtless; to that Monarch Whose dwelling is the light of seven days, and Who charges

His angels with folly. Judge and Monarch
—we may fasten attention overweeningly on
those aspects of God's being, and we shall
feel that Holiness so tenacious and Sovereignty so lonely will never embrace us in
their arms or admit us to their secret. Between them and us a great gulf is fixed.
From His farther side He may pity our hap-
less exile, and from our hither side we may
yearn for friendly access to Him; but
this will be all. The Monarch may not
stoop to our rags and penury, and the
Judge must condemn our evil.

"But," says Christ, "your portrait of
God is incomplete and inexact. It exag-
gerates certain features of His soul and
certain phases of His activity. It forgets
other features and phases. He is not only
Judge and Monarch. He is nearer, gentler,
homelier, more familiar. He is Father. It
is *your Father's* good pleasure to give you
the kingdom." Let the meaning and music
of the name be our amulet, our cordial,
and our cure. Mr. Lowell thinks that, if
only you could find " a perfectly wise and
perfectly good despot, such as the world

has never seen, except in the white-haired king of the poet, who ' lived long ago, in the morning when earth was nearer heaven than now,' " his presence and rule would be best for everybody. But fatherhood is more than the choicest despotism, and especially the One Fatherhood which is " perfectly wise and perfectly good." God is Father; and, whatever His statelinesses and awfulnesses are, a heart of passion and love pulses behind them. He is Father; and He spared not His Own Son, but delivered Him up for us. He is Father; and nothing but mercy prompts the sharpest trial He sends for our refining and perfecting. He is Father; and necessity compels Him to fill His kingdom with happy citizens: He must gather round Him the sons and daughters of the family. Our fears will spread their dusky wings and fly, when we spell out the theology and the religion, the relief and the tenderness, of the Father's grace.

IV

Once again: There is the fear that proceeds

from the presentiment of obstacles and hindrances ; but Christ dispels it by reminding us of the victoriousness of grace.

He calls the disciples a *little flock*. Sheep and lambs are defenceless creatures. In the grip of the wild beasts that rush from lair and covert, before the spears of the robbers sallying out from their caves among the hills, what can they do ? They are so frequently their own worst enemies, for they have little of the sagacity which protects other animals. Furthermore, the flock of God is never conspicuously large. In every age and country it has been surrounded by dispiriting masses of insensibility and unbelief, dislike and alienation, selfishness and sin. It is difficult for its members, with the prowling wolves threatening them, with the atmosphere more subtly or more aggressively unfriendly, and with their own palpable stupidities and errors, to be confident that the kingdom is theirs meantime and will be theirs to all eternity.

But over against the flock is the shepherd, to guard the sheep from adversaries outside and from their frailties within, and to convoy them step by step and mile after mile to an unassailable fold—the Shepherd Who, in this instance, is the Lord God Almighty. *He shall feed His flock; He shall gather the lambs with His arm, and carry them in His bosom.* Mr. George Trevelyan relates an incident of Garibaldi's life on the Island of Caprera. One evening the party in the house heard that a new-born lamb had been lost among the rocks. Long search by candle-light, over the crags and through the brushwood, failed of success. " It was nine o'clock and raining, and we were very tired," one of them says ; " so we returned to the house, and went to bed. An hour afterwards, we heard the sound of footsteps in the next room, and the front door opened. About midnight we were roused by a voice. It was Garibaldi returning, carrying the lost lamb in his arms. He took the little creature to his own bed, and lay down with it, giving it a bit of sponge dipped in milk to keep it quiet ; and he spent the whole night caressing and feeding it." It is a far-off parable of the conquests and consummations of God's love and grace. Let us repose in Him simply and always; and, though obstacles " seem like prison-walls to be," He will bring us to, and He will keep us in, the kingdom which cannot be moved.

XVII

ECCLESIOLA DEI

THE Latin is Philip Melanchthon's,
and means "God's Little Church."
That New Testament Apostle at whose feet
Melanchthon sat, and never wearied listening
and learning, had his own older version of
it, *The Church that is in the House*. The
phrase, alike in its first and in its sixteenth
century accent, assures us that our Holy
Place does not require any pilgrimage to
bring us to its threshold. The room or
the kitchen, where we are every day, should
be synagogue and temple and shrine. The
fact is, that neither Master Philip nor the
Apostle of the Gentiles can claim that the
assurance had its origin with him. It is
much more ancient. The Old Testament
anticipates them both. It sounds the praises
of God's Little Church.

I

To start with, there is the reasonableness of family religion.

Joshua, his marches and battles done, clings to the loyalties of his youth. He registers his vow—*As for me and my house, we will serve the Lord* (Joshua xxiv. 15). In the court of reflection, and at the bar of conscience, it is a vow which needs no defence; its rightness and its goodness are evident. The patriot should bind himself by it; for only the pieties of home will guarantee the security of the commonwealth and the truest and highest liberty of the people. The Christian should subscribe to it; he knows that the faith's most intelligent and most indefatigable soldiers come from hearths and inglenooks where the altar of God is kept in repair. The lover of the children should endorse it; their chiefest treasure is that holy familiarity with the Lord of heaven and earth which makes Him " a Presence felt the livelong day, a welcome Fear at night "—not money, nor the illumination of the schools, nor the world's countenance and commendation. Joshua's oath should be sworn by all wise men. It is rational, obligatory, worthy.

II

Again, there is the orderliness of family religion.

It should have method in it. It should have system. Professor Dowden portrays George Herbert as poet of a spirituality "which accepts and is assisted by rule and habit." The recurrences are never merely formal and mechanical; the flowers growing in the garden are living flowers; but Herbert is certain that they flourish best, and show most comely, when they are bedded in definite patterns, and watered through accustomed and regular channels. Indeed, the saint and singer of Bemerton has wisdom on his side. Here is David. He has his throne to establish, and the Ark to lead to its sanctuary; but something else occupies him too. *Then David returned to bless his household* (2 Samuel vi. 20). State affairs and anxieties for the Tabernacle must not break the periodicities and punctualities, the rhythm and refrain, of this more private devotion. Those wholesome periodicities—our ancestors honoured them more than we. The morning and the evening sacrifice is rarer in our homes. Certainly, modern conditions of life are unpropitious. The haste of business, the early hour at which some of us must be out and away, the difficulty of assembling all for even a few minutes ; these are serious obstacles. But it is worth taking pains to give visibility and discipline to that godliness which, surely, we wish to permeate the dwelling that draws and holds and charms us like a magnet. "When I came first to Kidderminster," wrote Richard Baxter, " there was about one family that worshipped God and called on His Name ; and, when I came away, there were streets where not one poor family in a side did not do so." So gracious an orderliness we should covet and copy.

III

Then there is the fruitfulness of family religion.

From David and Joshua we travel back

to the grey fathers of the world. *I know Abraham*, God said, *that he will command his children, and they shall keep the way of the Lord* (Genesis xviii. 19). The reverence, the trustfulness, and the grace of Abraham's tent will not die with Abraham, but will be repeated by those whom he has influenced so mightily. Of course, there are exceptions. Some are nurtured in the midst of saintliness, and they wander far and hopelessly. Others, against whom fate seemed to fight from the cradle, are found by the Good Shepherd Who is stronger than all bad heredities. But, usually, the faith of the home lives on through subsequent generations. There is an amazing power in memory ; the recollections of the past rise up after the lapse of years. There is a boundless virtue in example ; the impression of a dedicated life is seldom lost. There is an extraordinary vitality in love ; when its seeds are sown ungrudgingly and profusely, it bears its harvest after many days. There is an indestructible music in the Gospel ; its strains, once heard, are apt to pursue us to the last. " This Name of my Saviour, Thy Son," cries St. Augustine—

the Augustine who wandered far and long from Monica's hearth and the God Who fed its fires—"had my tender heart drunk in even with my mother's milk; and whatsoever was without this Name, though never so erudite, polished, and truthful, took not complete hold of me." It is a fruitfulness which has durable and perennial returns.

IV

And there is the present gladness of family religion.

The Lord blessed the house of Obed-Edom because of the Ark (2 Samuel vi. 12). The grass grew greener round the happy house. The wheels ran more smoothly within its walls. I do not affirm that the altar at the fireside, and the veneration by the inmates of the home of the Ark of the Covenant, will be passport and fee to procure material riches and external triumphs, though the practice of religion does clarify the brain and breathe decision into the will and impart energy to the arm. But there is a better wealth. Those whose praises have gone up to God in unison, and whose petitions and requests are such as Mr. Whittier describes—

> Heart answers heart; in one desire
> The blending lines of prayer aspire

—they have a great reward. This is how they win the spirit of mutual forbearance, patience, helpfulness, affection. This is how they are baptized with strength, for their common duties; with humility, so that in their common successes they are restrained from pride; with comfort, that in their common sorrows they may not faint or fail. God draws near them, to abide in their fellowship and to satisfy their souls. Like the Gittite, they inhabit the Field of the Blessed Man.

V

Once more, there is the final profitableness of family religion.

Jeremiah has a fragrant oracle : *I will take you, two of a family, and I will bring you to Zion* (Jeremiah iii. 14). Not as isolated units and strangers, but in little groups of those who are closely related and dear, the exiles were to say good-bye to the tyrannies of heathen Babylon, and to cross the great barren spaces of the desert, and to enter again the old home ; and the thought would add a keener joy to the prospect of restoration. It is still God's promise : *Two of a family I will bring you to Zion.* The Zion of a purer world than this. The Jerusalem which stands conjubilant with song. The city in which there is neither night, nor death, nor sin, nor curse. To discover ourselves in it, alone, would be a wonder of wonders. But to have beside us those we knew best and loved most, and hand in hand with them to follow Christ, will be even more desirable. " There is not room enough," writes William Cowper to his cousin, Lady Hesketh, " for friendship to unfold itself in full bloom in such a nook of life as this. Therefore, I am, and must, and will be, yours for ever." To this end of ends let us point our children and our kinsfolk. As much as in us lies, let us aid them to reach it, and set their feet in the road that runs rom God's little Chu ch to God's Church exultant in the heavens.

XVIII

UP THE STAIR

THAT much-rhymed and rhyme-worthy little brother, the lark, has had many immortal numbers dedicated to him; but the remembrance of the best of them cannot cloy the first-hand perfection of a living poet's[1] tribute:

> There was no bird: only a singing,
> Up in the glory, climbing and ringing,
> Like a small golden cloud at even,
> Trembling 'twixt earth and heaven.
>
> I saw no staircase winding, winding,
> Up in the dazzle, sapphire and blinding;
> Yet round by round, in exquisite air,
> The song went up the stair.

"This is so accurate and faithful," writes Miss Louise Imogen Guiney, "that it need not ever be superseded; and its cunning

[1] Mrs. Katharine Tynan Hinkson in *The Wind in the Trees.*

166

accidental value is that it is literature."
Now, the Book of Isaiah paints an exactly
similar picture of the life which pleases God
(lxiv. 5)—*Thou meetest him that rejoiceth and
worketh righteousness, those that remember
Thee in Thy ways.* Let us watch the stair
mounting higher, flight upon flight, from one
gracious endowment to another. Let us
hear the heart's song as it goes up, round
by round, story after story, to the gladness
of a fellowship too intimate and too enriching ever to be broken.

I

The life to which we are called starts
—where, indeed, the text ends—with Remembrance. *Those that remember Thee in
Thy ways* are on the first step of the ladder.

So God is now Centre and Pivot of our
system. Self is dethroned, whether the
reasoning Self that schemed out our salvation, or the proud Self that hated to submit
to the will of Another, or the despairing
Self which feared that neither in earth nor
in heaven could a remedy be found for our

sin. These have vanished, and He fills our horizon. We are sure of His necessity, His sufficingness, and His over-overcoming grace.

And it is God's disclosed character and practical loving activity which attract us most. Theorizings and dreams about His essential Being we must leave in large measure alone ; they are too high for us. But we observe Him in His *ways*, as He emerges from the thick darkness and the overpowering splendour to bless us and do us good. There is One, especially, Who is His Way. I behold Christ travelling steadfastly to the Cross, and dying freely there for the forgiveness of sinful men ; and I know God's Way of pardon. I see Christ return to the eternal priesthood and kingship of the Throne ; and I understand God's Way of wealthy supply and perfect peace. I receive and cherish Christ, in the Person of the Spirit Who is His Deputy and Representative ; and, week in and week out, I am conversant with God's Way of holiness and power. This manifestation of God in Jesus Christ, these saving and comforting and sanctifying energies of His, are our daily study, our daily marvel, and our daily bread.

Yes, our daily study. The prophet speaks of *remembering* the Divine ways; and we have to make silences in the stridency and bustle, we have to clear a space in the crowded and chattering scene, for the blessed work. There are saints who, as often as the minute-hand on the dial of their watches enters upon a new hour, have schooled themselves to a thought of God, or to a brief prayer, or to the mental repetition of a verse from the Holy Word. Whether we follow their rules or no, we must accustom ourselves to the habit of Recollection, and we must practise the Presence. From almost anywhere on the wide spaces of the Moor of Rannoch, or on the long stretch of the Loch, if the weather is fair, you can see the glorious cone of Schiehallion far above you against the sky. Thus, in every spot and circumstance of life, we may see the climbing ridges and snow-capped peaks of God's Ways and gather fresh inspiration from the sight. But we must shut ourselves alone with Him. We must pause and remember.

II

That is the first flight of the stair. The next is Joy. *Him that rejoiceth*, the prophet says.

For God is not only the Centre of our system; He ought to be the Rapture and Refreshment of our soul. Many people find their joys away from Him, in the rush of business, in the gaieties of amusement, in books and pictures, even in the indulgence of favourite sin. To have continually recurring glimpses of His holiness, and to face His claims on themselves would, they are sure, sap and kill their pleasure; and they dismiss Him from their world as much as they can. You and I sympathized with them once; but we have no shred of sympathy with them to-day. Like Henry Martyn, in those last hours at Tokat, we think "with sweet peace of our God; in solitude our Company, our Friend, and our Comforter."

Well, but are we joyful enough? Christians let the wear and tear of their tasks, and their petty annoyances, and their crushing griefs interfere mischievously with their inner calmness and triumph. We imagine that joy is a kind of luxury, a sort of extra, to which only the happy minority may aspire; whereas it is the command for every one. "Put sadness away from thee," says an early writing, *The Shepherd of Hermas*; "array thee in the joy that finds favour in God's sight; yea, revel thou therein. For every one that is joyous worketh and thinketh those things that are good. But he that is sad doeth wickedly; he worketh lawlessness, in that he neither prayeth to God nor giveth Him thanks. For sadness is the sister of half-heartedness and bitterness." There is shrewd spiritual counsel, and some of us have great need to ponder it.

The Joy is child of the Remembrance. If I take time to meditate on God's ways in Christ, forgiving, cleansing, keeping, empowering, perfecting; how He and no other has assumed the control; how He begins and performs the good work: there will be quietness in my heart; there will be buoyancy in my step; and my features will carry on them what old Matthew Roydon describes quaintly and engagingly—

171

> A sweet attractive kinde of grace,
> A full assurance given by lookes,
> Continuall comfort in a face,
> The lineaments of gospell-bookes.

This is what God ought to get from me.
This only is a true report of Him, and His
dear Son, and His fertile land.

III

There is the ladder's second stage. The
third is Obedience. The verse commemo-
rates *him that worketh righteousness*.

Obedience has its roots. They are just
those great motives we have been passing
in review, Remembrance and Joy. We are
not likely to serve, willingly or effectively
or untiringly, One Who is a comparative
stranger, and, still less, One of Whom we
are suspicious and afraid. But when we have
a clear vision of, and a constant delight in,
God's actings and sufferings and givings
through our Lord and Saviour, Jesus Christ
—for this Master, Who is Friend as much as
Master, we run and are not weary, and we
walk and do not faint. The " very thinking

of the thought gives light to know, and life to do, and marvellous strength to bear." The winter of our misconception and discontent is gone, and the springtime of our consecration is ushered in.

Then Obedience has its flower—the flower which the prophet designates Righteousness. When the new life commenced, God, without merit of ours, attired us from head to foot in Christ's righteousness; and, for His sake, we stood justified before the Eyes which are as a flame of fire. Now, day after day, more and more, we are changed ourselves into the texture and tenor, the bloom and perfume, of our Lord's righteousness. Towards both God and our neighbour we learn to hate the things that are unholy, and to love the things that are true and pure and of good report. It is not an emotion merely, or an abstract conviction of the brain. Him that *worketh* righteousness : this is the peremptory and strenuous word. I proclaim it with the lips. I contend for it in the life. I show it in little matters and in great, that men may glorify my Father Who is in heaven. Yet it is never irksome or a drudgery. As the bondservants surrender themselves morning by morning to their Lord, He strengthens them by His Spirit in the inner man, and in His will is their peace, and obedience spells liberty.

IV

This is the third step of the stair. We are ready for the goal. It is Communion, realized, close, heart-filling, inexpressible. *Thou meetest him*, says the verse.

We have the Communion at each separate stage of the ascent. When we remember God's ways towards ourselves, He meets us in Fatherhood and grace. When His dealings in salvation fill us with a joy we cannot hide, He meets us still more un-ambiguously. When in the pursuit and pro-secution of actual righteousness we work for Him, and hate even the garment spotted by the flesh, He meets us most largely and endearingly; He and we walk together, and are agreed; love, in the haunting words of a prince in the Church, has made one spirit out of two.

174

But the ultimate goal is in front. It is where the lark and its music are, when they have attained their noblest estate—

Up in the dazzle, sapphire and blinding.

We shall see Christ face to face ; and His Father and ours will dwell with us in that city from which we shall go no more out. This is the top of the staircase, and the end of ends, and the best of bests. Wonderful—is it not ?—that such a meeting and communion should be reserved for such men and women as we. And having these hopes, what manner of persons ought we to be in all holy conversation and godliness !

XIX

A BROKEN AND EMPTIED VESSEL

ST. PAUL has been boasting. It is work to which he is unaccustomed, and which he greatly dislikes. The Corinthians have forced him to it. They are endangering the Gospel through slights which they have cast on himself, the evangelist of the Gospel. They are compelling Christ to suffer because they heap scorn on Christ's messenger. For his Lord's sake he has had to face and perform the distasteful task of publishing his own credentials. But he gets back, as soon as possible, to the accents which are habitual with him, and which regeneration has made his native dialect. *Though I be nothing*, he writes (2 Corinthians xii. 11) ; and there we listen to the Paul who, with undisguised sincerity, called himself less than the least of all saints, and the chief of sinners.

A BROKEN AND EMPTIED VESSEL

" It is as difficult to be humble," says
Mary Coleridge in her Diary, "as it is easy
to despair. Despair's a very conceited
thing ; but I might as well hope to be
Michael Angelo as to be humble. The
grace of the lowliest is given only to the
highest." Moses in the Old Testament,
and Paul in the New, are highest of Biblical
men, and to these princes of the chariot the
grace of the lowliest was given. They
are unaffectedly humble. God translate
us into their image !

I

Though I be nothing. The words fit us
well. They are the confession of the
creature.

Man as man seems trivial, seems nothing.
There is the shortness of his life. The
French verse describes it—

> La vie est brève ;
> Un peu d'espoir,
> Un peu de rêve . . .
> Et puis, Bon soir !—

a little hoping, a little dreaming, and then,

Good Night! There is the limitation of his knowledge. Take the masters of science; and the tiny circle of their light is compassed round by a wider circle of mist and haze, dubieties and guesses and conjectures, about which they dare make no certain affirmations; ay, and this again is set in a still vaster circle where all is dark, ominous, unexplored. And there is the meagreness of his achievement. He may not be an idler or a dilatory looker-on. Early and late he is at his post. But there are innumerable hindrances, disadvantageous circumstances, difficulties and delays. He requires a larger canvas for his picture. He needs an ampler time in which to finish his work. He has to rise and go, when the execution of his purposes is little more than begun.

Because we are creatures, we are nothing. Yet do not let us be sour, cynical, rebellious, because our age is a hand-breadth, our knowledge infinitesimal, our attainments broken, our victories scarcely better than half-defeats. No, but let us learn how imperative it is that we should flee to God, and should draw our strength and resource from

Him. The sense of our impotence is to humble us into the realization that He is indispensable. And when we are ground to powder in our own esteem and betake ourselves in poverty and helplessness to the Father of our spirits, what a change ensues! He breathes His immortality into our brittle natures; and we are destined to a life beyond life, conscious, personal, fruitful, triumphant. He introduces us to the knowledge which is profoundest, and which grows from more to more through an everlasting future. He communicates a new vigour and value to our labours, so that they are not in vain in the Lord, but have far-travelling issues, and the heavenly period perfects the earthen. When our nothingness sends us hungrily, clingingly, and appropriatingly to the fullness of God, we become rich and enduring.

II

Though I be nothing. The words suit us. They are the cry of the sinner.

The sinner—when his subterfuges and plausibilities are bared and exposed, when his easy indifference and his proud self-trust have both been undermined, and when he abhors himself. There are no depths too abysmal for such a soul; there is no indictment too heavy. As a creature a man may recognize that he is nothing; but as a sinner he stands afar off, and beats on his breast, and cries out that he is nothing, with a poignancy and sorrow and self-abasement of which he had no inkling before. There is something positive, something active, something unsparing, in his obliteration and repudiation of himself now. Our creatureliness makes us bow our heads; but our sinnership lays us in the very dust.

Suppose we see ourselves confronted with the Law of God. It demands a fleckless obedience. Faced by its *Thou shalts*, we are overwhelmingly aware of the demerit of our sin. We discover that we are guilty, and deserving indeed of the second death. Or suppose we see ourselves contrasted with the Character of God. He is Light of light. He is Purity most pure. He is whiter than the petals of the lily, than the foam which crests the tumbling wave, than the virgin snow on the shining summit of the Alp. Beholding Him, we are cognizant of the shame of our sin. It has befouled us. It has made us lovers of the darkness rather than of the noonday. Or suppose we see ourselves disqualified for the Gift of God. It is the gift of peace—a conscience quiet, a heart at rest, a will running the way of the commandments, the nature within unruffled like nature without on the morning of Christ's Nativity, when " birds of calm sat brooding on the charmed wave." But the wretchedness of our sin ! It has thrown our being out of tune. It has dowered us with accusations and dreads. It has robbed us of peace.

So we, sinners, are nothing. We are worse than nothing—a blot, a disfigurement, a contradiction of God's purpose, a grief to His inmost soul. But if the mournful fact has been burned into us by the searching Word and the revealing Spirit, shall we give up everything for lost ? By no means. Our very extremity is the reason why we should repair to God in Christ. Our sin is demerit ; but in the dying Christ there is merit to atone for its most hideous guilt. Our sin is shame; but in the living Christ there is power to wash the leper's flesh till it is sweet as a little child's. Our sin is wretchedness; but in the indwelling Christ there is the secret of peace. From the " I," who is nothing, let us betake ourselves to the " Thou," Who is Everything.

Mr. Verrall has a fine and moving essay on the dream of the poet Statius, in his *Thebaid*, about the Altar of Mercy. In the midst of the city of Athens the Altar was built. Mercy there had fixed her seat, and misery made it holy. New suppliants were ever coming to it, and ever finding acceptance—shaking fear, and shivering poverty; the conquered and the exile; fallen power, and wandering wickedness. The ritual took no tax, accepted no incense-flame, insisted on no drench of blood, but asked only the dew of tears upon the stone. And to entreat was to be heard; and, both in the dark and in the light, all hours gave access to one whose grace cost nothing but a complaint. The beautiful dream of Statius is the simple certainty of the Gospel. The

Altar of Mercy is the Christ of Calvary, of the heavenly place, of individual experience. We come to Him labouring and heavy laden, and He gives us rest. We come to Him nothing, and henceforth He is our All.

III

Though I be nothing. The words should be dear to us. They are the conviction of the saint.

We continue paupers at our Father's door to the last. We are debtors to our Good Physician until our dying hour. *Though I be nothing*, said St. Paul, the prince of apostles ; for still he was persuaded of his emptiness, and still he went on drawing from the soundless wells in his Lord. Let us be Pauline Christians here as elsewhere, for the maturest of us is undone without Christ's abiding Life and Holy Spirit. Is it your own personality ? You will soon be at the mercy of former sins, you will soon be a prey to restlessness, you will lose your influence and your fragrance, if you let yourself imagine that you are something and somebody, and can venture in any measure to dispense with your divine Keeper. Is it your speech and work on the behalf and in the vineyard of the Master? These may be brilliant, arresting, effective after a fashion. But they will be cold, they will not move and melt, if you are yourself the artificer of what you say and do. You must not miss the unction from on High. There is no advance, there is no prosperity, apart from that.

But, when it is our daily prayer, "Let me be forgotten and crucified, and pour Thou Thyself into me," Christ in us repeats His former miracles, and does yet greater works than these. He, inhabiting us in His sufficient Spirit, is our Sanctification and Fountain of supply. He, employing our speech and our labour, accomplishes the good pleasure of His will. Hard by Robert Bruce's church in Larbert was a room where he spent his time between sermons. One day the congregation wondered why he delayed to come out from the room for the second diet of worship. The attendant was sent to inquire. At the door he halted, for he heard a conversation going on within. He returned to report that there was Some One in the vestry with the minister ; that Master Bruce was saying many times, and with much emphasis, that he could not go alone into the church, but must have the Other with him ; and that, as yet, the Other answered him never a word. This invisible, mysterious, all-prevalent, infinite Some One—the Lord Who is the Wisdom of God and the Power of God to us who believe in Him : we dare not take a step without Him. Unless He goes with us, we are nothing, we are less than nothing and vanity. When He goes, we can do all, and we have all and abound.

XX

MAN'S WEAKNESS LEANING
UPON GOD

IN that marvellous initial vision, which
transformed the prophet himself and
everything around him, Ezekiel was made
aware of four living creatures who fulfilled
the errands of the Most High Lord. They
symbolize the men and women whom God
can employ in the sacred services of His
kingdom; you and I may be these mystic
and conquering messengers of His. *And
every one had four faces, and every one had
four wings* (Ezekiel i. 6). What does the
sentence mean? As I take it, it means that
the natural in us must be caught up into
the spiritual, the earthly multiplied by the
heavenly, the human sublimed and revolu-
tionized through the divine. The faces
belong to the lower world; they are those

of a man, a lion, an ox, and an eagle
—common faces enough. But the wings
suggest the upper world. They are Jehovah's wings, sheltering, almighty, holy.
They move, they throb, they soar, in the
region of the supersensual. You see the
lesson. Our strength is weakness, until it
leans on God. Without His wings, to bear
us up and to carry us forward, we can do
nothing. With them impelling and master-
ing us, we do all things.

I

The intelligence of the mind is unavailing,
unless the Spirit of God directs it.

The living creature, with the face of a man
—he is emblem of reason and thought; the
logic which supposes itself furnished and prepared to solve every difficulty; the scrutiny of
the near and the far ; the probing and dis-
covering and triumphant mind. What will
not the intellect of man attempt ? What
has it not achieved ? It looks as if soon no
more secrets would be left for it to unravel
and no new territories to annex. And this
clever and assertive intelligence is apt to

conclude that, in the spiritual sphere, nothing is required beyond its ingenuity and resource. If my Christian life lags and falters in a kind of Babylonian captivity, can I not devise my own recovery and reinforcement ? If the world is out of joint, and men round about me are enmeshed in sin and misery, it should be possible by inquiry and study and the expedients of philanthropic enterprise to evolve an adequate scheme of amendment and reform. But no ! these are questions too big, too serious, and too appalling. In front of them the mind has to lower its proud flag and to confess its inability and defeat.

There is another Mind to Whose wisdom we must bow, Whose conclusions we must accept, and Whose mandates we must obey, when we are in the realm of souls. It is not that we are to abjure our own thinking ; never should we be more awake than here and now ; but it is that our thinking must be in subjection to God's truth and command. I may familiarize myself with all the aids to personal religion which are within my reach ; but in the end I must trust the Holy Ghost to rectify what is amiss in me, and to lead me forward from stage to stage. I may set my brains to investigate the world's necessity and to provide alleviations and anodynes, replies to its troublesome questions and remedies for its grievous wound; but my chief assets, if I am to benefit perishing men, are faith in the crucified and risen Christ, and intercessory prayer to Him. Let us acknowledge that our intelligence can travel a very short way. Let us be sure that round and above the face of man are the Wings of God.

II

The courage of the soul is futile, too, unless the Spirit of God inspires it.

The living creature's second face was a lion's; and the lion is type of daring and dreadlessness. *The lion hath roared*, says Amos the herdsman, *who will not fear?* Indeed, it is good to have the lion-heart. The more towering the obstacle, the more frowning the foe, the more eager some of us are to attack them. There is a positive invitation in their threatening aspect, a

189

trumpet-call in the boldness with which they stride across our path. When the very hills seemed watching with hostile eyes, and a weird and awesome noise was everywhere, and the lost adventurers stood round to see the last of him, the poet's hero set his horn dauntlessly to his lips, and blew, " Childe Roland to the Dark Tower came." May be, we sympathize with Childe Roland's stern joy.

Yet the bravery is quite too little, when the Dark Tower which has to be subdued, and changed into a palace of light and liberty, is our own heart, or our neighbour's character, or the world that lies in the wicked one. The stoutest courage is unequal to adventures like these. We cannot rid ourselves of sin. We cannot infuse a new spirit into Christless souls. The love of the Father, the grace of the Saviour, and the communion of the Holy Ghost are the indispensable endowments ; and without them the boldest is certain to be put to shame. Our hardihood is helpless. Our " furious force " is emasculated and baffled before those malign presences, as the " furious force " of the king of beasts was amazed and forgotten before the unarmed sweetness and holiness of Una in the forest. Not on the lion's face can we depend, but only on God's Wings and God Himself.

III

And the patient endurance of the will is unsuccessful, unless the Spirit of God sustains it.

Here is the ox's face; and the ox is parable and portrait of plodding toil. It has not the lion's spring and rush and audacity; but it has what is better, the quality of steady continuance in unassuming work. " As far as runs the fallow, as late as holds the light," it bows its neck meekly to the yoke, and treads the furrows of the field; and its modest and unremarked labour secures the harvest and blesses men. The toilers who abide by an inconspicuous post, and do not dream of forsaking the tiring and monotonous claylands, are loved and honoured of God. In His kingdom we do not usually reap quick returns. The delays are long ; and there is much need for the enduring will that is not drawn aside or persuaded to desist.

But there can be no such prosecution of His tasks apart from the reception of His grace. Our resolve, and lofty conception of duty, are not enough. Is it the full assurance of personal salvation, or the perfecting of our own Christliness, that we covet ? Is it the regeneration of a child or a friend ? Is it the revival of the Church, when its life halts and declines ? Is it the ingathering of the wandering nations to the Shepherd's fold ? Unobtrusively we go on, hungering and praying for these heavenly ends. But they are beyond us. However unintermitted our endeavour, however limitless our patience, we must rely on Another. It is the Lord Who keeps us from losing heart. It is the Lord Who sees that in due season we reap if we faint not. It is the Lord Who, at the close of the day, will surprise us with gifts and benedictions exceeding abundant above what we asked or thought. "Behind the plough the Christ is—with me behind the plough." To the panting ox what a difference the uplifting and unflagging Wings of God make !

IV

And the hopes of the heart are cheated, unless the Spirit of God fans them.

The living creature has a fourth face, an eagle's ; and the eagle is sign and summary of aspiration. He mounts above the mists. He is citizen of an ampler air.

> Close to the sun in lonely lands,
> Ringed with the azure world, he stands.
> The wrinkled sea beneath him crawls ;
> He watches from his mountain walls.

Among exhilarations, exuberances, exaltations the eagle lives. It means much for you and me to abound in hope ; and the optimist undertakes and performs more than the pessimist. But a merely human hope, a sanguine disposition, the habit of seeing the glad and bright aspect of things, will not carry us far in the spiritual world. Our hopes for the progress of the kingdom of righteousness and peace will be buffeted and broken, if they are not maintained in liveliness by the blessed Spirit of God. Within and without, it has such opposing winds and contrary tides to meet, such a dead weight of indifference, such worldliness, such an infatuation for pleasure, such deep-entrenched opinions and customs, that, left to himself, the most valiant and inveterate optimist among us must succumb to despondency. It is God Who drives the fatal accidie away, and strengthens us never to despair.

There are wings and wings, the wings of an eagle and the Wings of the Lord. The former may bear us aloft and sustain us in many a storm, but they are liable to droop and fail. I did not finish Tennyson's fragment:

> He watches from his mountain walls,
> And like a thunderbolt he falls.

Well, the descent may be voluntary, the swoop of an untrammelled freedom, the proud foray of the reaver and robber, the mercilessness of a tyrant rejoicing to deal out death. But sometimes, both with the eagle and with the heart of man, the descent is involuntary. We are driven to it against our desire. We are battered with the shocks of doom, and smitten at last to the ground, our foresight balked, and all our expectations crushed and slain. But the Wings of the Lord are never worn out. Neither death nor life, nor angels nor principalities nor powers, nor things present nor things to come, nor height nor depth, nor any other creature, can destroy the hopes He begets in us. For they are hopes which are founded on the purpose of the Father, on the redemption and resurrection and endless life of the Son, and on the omnipotence and indestructible grace of the Spirit.

XXI

TIME'S WINGED CHARIOT

" I NEVER knew any man "—it is Dr.
John Brown who is portraying his
father—" who lived more truly under the
power, and sometimes under the shadow,
of the world to come. This world had to
him little reality, except as leading to the
next ; little interest, except as the time of
probation and sentence. A child brought
to him to be baptized was in his mind, and
in his words, ' a young immortal to be
educated for eternity.' A birth was the
beginning of what was never to end. . . .
When oppressed with this feeling — the
hurry of mankind out of this brief world
into the unchangeable next—I have heard
him, with deep emotion, repeat Andrew
Marvell's strong lines,

But at my back I always hear
Time's wingèd chariot hurrying near ;
And yonder all before me lie
Deserts of vast Eternity."

It is the right attitude. It is the Christian
view. Perhaps, in this instance, the
element of sadness was unduly prominent ;
the son is describing a father whose temperament was tinged with melancholy. We
are not called to live under the shadow of the
world to come. But, beyond all debate, we
are called to live under its power.

Three times the Greek adjective *proskairos* is used in the New Testament. The
pleasures of sin are *for a season* (Hebrews
xi. 25). The good seed, which has not
a sufficient grip of the earth, endures *for a
while* (Matthew xiii. 21). The things that
are seen are *temporal*, or, to borrow a parallel
expression from the same passage, *for a
moment* (2 Corinthians iv. 18). That which
lingers for a season, and thrives for a while,
and lasts for a moment : it is the sum-total
of the possessions of many. But over
against those short-sighted souls are the
wiser souls, who covet and claim that which

abides and grows for ever and ever. God grant that we may choose this better part !

I

There is an enjoyment which is transitory. Sin has its pleasures. They are both genuine and generous. They have an appetizing flavour, a luscious sweetness, a seductive appeal. Whether the attraction of evil is for the body, or for the intellect, or for the spirit, it is a positive and intense attraction. There is tingling delight in letting the senses take the reins, and carry us wherever they please, down into forbidden things and away into the far country. There are glamour and gladness in the unrestricted play of the mental powers and the successful assertion of the self-life, although these are divorced from God and from goodness, as they were in giants like Goethe and Napoleon. There are quiet, untroubled, proud days and nights for the spirit, so long as it imagines that it is amply equipped for its own preservation and progress, and discards the grace that is superhuman and divine.

But these are imaginations we shall not contrive to keep up always. Sin's pleasure is *proskairos — for a season*. The season may run its course with a lightning rapidity. The enticement of bodily indulgence is apt to vanish suddenly, and the eyes are opened, and men know that they have reaped a bitter harvest. Or the season may be longer. Napoleon's Elba and St. Helena are postponed for years. A man dies in the spiritual arrogance which dispenses with God in Christ. But then death is the commencement rather than the close of life ; and, after it, the disillusionment and the deluge follow. The Gospels speak, in a tremendous phrase, of *eternal sin*. And eternal sin is sin without any pleasures in it. It is sin which is conscious bondage, but from which the soul is helpless to escape. It is misery unrelieved and immeasurable.

So let me prefer, as Moses preferred, *the people of God*. They may have no form or comeliness, as their Master seemed to have none. But God has bought them with a costly price, and He guards them with a jealous care. They are His children, and the fellow-heirs with His First-born Son. There is nothing transitory about them; they are stamped with His Own everlastingness. If I am among them, I sing, "While God and I shall be, I am His and He is mine."

II

There is a religion which is evanescent.

I suppose that, here and there, human beings may be found who are quite without religion—materialists, unvisited by a quickening glimpse of the supersensual world, or by a passing wish for some kindlier and heavenlier realm than that of the actual; and atheists, whose denial of God is unreserved and complete. But the materialists and the atheists are, happily, a much smaller company than the people who designate themselves by the mournful names. The peril besetting most of us is not that we shall strip ourselves of all religion but that we shall be satisfied with its simulacrum and husk. The hearers of the rocky ground welcome the good seed, but they are too shallow to hold it fast, and to give it depth and room that it may bear its proper fruit. They dure *for a while*, but only for a while. Their religion may be mainly a stirring of the emotions; they are melted, moved, lifted above themselves. Or it is a reliance on what is outwardly right and seemly and sacred; and this, too, is praiseworthy, an asset of value, and a safeguard never to be despised. But in both cases the man is *proskairos*, one whose goodness is no more permanent than the morning cloud and the early dew. Emotions have to be translated into the trust that is lifelong, the love which is the deepest and highest thing in the nature, and the loyalty that refuses to swerve; or how soon they will be dissipated! Custom and observance must be of the essence of the soul; or they will shrivel into nothingness before the brightness of Christ's appearing. "Jerusalem the earthly," writes Mr. Stephen Graham, "is a pleasure-ground for wealthy sightseers, and a place where every stone has been commercialised by tourist agencies or by greedy monks." That is not the Jerusalem which is above, which is true, and which will remain when sun and moon are blotted out. But when the traveller adds : "In my heart was a little compass-box where an arrow always pointed steadily to Jerusalem," we catch a gleam of the better and more lasting City. And may God lodge in our hearts the arrow which always points steadily to this supreme Jerusalem!

Yes, instead of the soil that is superficial and the religion that is evanescent, let me crave the honest and prepared heart, taught of the Holy Spirit, which takes the living Word to itself, and meditates upon it, and prays over it, and submits to it day after day. Here is the secret of growth in the grace and knowledge of our Lord and Saviour. Here is the nourishment of a life which goes from strength to strength, till it appears before God in Zion, to behold His face in righteousness and to be satisfied for ever and ever with His likeness.

III

Finally, there is a world which is perishing.

The things which are seen, says St. Paul.

He is thinking, not so much of Nature—
the green earth, and the round ocean, and
the living air, and the blue sky ; nor yet of
society—home, and Church, and State ;
but rather of that world which is inimical to
Christ and Christ's people. Pressure, and
perplexity, and persecution are in it ; down-
casting is in it, and the bearing about in the
body of the death of the Lord Jesus. Paul
was familiar with the storms that sweep
across its landscape, and the floods and
fires into which its inhabitants are plunged.
And, if we cleave to Christ through good
report and bad, we shall be familiar with
them also, although our griefs for the
Gospel's sake will not be so sharp or so
severe as his.

But the things which are seen are *pros-
kaira*. They are brief-lived, soon to be
removed. They last *for a moment*. The
affliction which is peculiar to the Christian
is in its essence so light and temporary
that it is not worth a thought in comparison
with the glory about to be revealed. That
is unending, infinite, inconceivable. That
will never fade. If it is our portion, why

should we be swallowed up of sorrow? We shall dwell in the House of the Lord, in the radiance of the Face of Christ, so long as the House stands and the Face shines.

Therefore, let me be absorbed in, and led captive by, the things which are unseen. Not that, like a recluse and hermit, I am to withdraw from the world round about me, but that all the contents of this world, its persons and its happenings, are to remind me of the other and refulgent world, which is my harbour and my goal. Eternity waits for me in the future ; but, as assuredly, eternity is within me just now—an eternity which should not be, in Andrew Marvell's phrase, a " desert " so much as an untrackable Paradise. It lives in me, and I in it, and everything I see and hear, or am called to do and to suffer, should suggest it to me. It is become my native air and spacious universe. And then, as the beautiful inscription in Londonderry Cathedral puts it,

'Twas but a step for those victorious feet
From their day's walk into the golden street

XXII

A SUNSHINE IN A SHADY PLACE

THAT true and patient scholar to whom lovers of the New Testament owe an immense debt, Bishop Lightfoot, has written an illuminating note on the *Domus Augusta* —the household of Cæsar. It was a vast household, not composed of members of the Imperial family, princes and princesses, courtiers and nobles, but filled with thousands of subordinates, who served in one capacity or in another the ruler of the world —slaves, or freedmen, or soldiers. They constituted a great part of the population, not only in Rome itself but throughout Italy and the Provinces. They fulfilled every sort of duty, more or less domestic : duties menial, duties of the poor and down-trodden drudge, duties replete with attrac-

205

tion and interest. But not one of them was his own master or mistress ; each was at the Emperor's beck and call, each must hurry on his errands and humour his caprices and lose his own individuality in his lord's. On the tombs which have been unearthed in or near the famous city on the Tiber, one may read who these men and women were and what they did. Then Bishop Lightfoot turns to the closing chapter of the Epistle to the Romans, with its greetings to this Christian and that other resident in the capital of the Empire, and shows that numbers of the names recorded there are identical with those in the sepulchral inscriptions — Amplias, Urbanus, Stachys, Apelles, Tryphæna and Tryphosa, Rufus, Hermes, Philologus and Julia. Working under Cæsar's orders and about his court, in the middle of the first century, were freedmen and slaves bearing these very designations. Probably they were the believers whom the Apostle remembered in so kindly a fashion. Probably, too, they were the saints who, when he was himself in Rome and in the midst of them, wished him to

convey their salutations to their brethren
in distant Philippi.

Saints that are of Cæsar's household
(Philippians iv. 22)—it is a graphic and
memorable phrase. Through the clouds
between us and them we may catch the
outline of their features and an echo of their
voices. They have a message for us, to which
we shall do well to listen.

I

This message: Saintliness dwells within,
but it ripens without.

How shall we define the saint? He is
one who, in his deepest being, is separated
to God and in covenant with Him. The
sun in his sky, the star Alcyone in his as-
tronomy, is God, Father and Saviour and
Spirit. From secret springs far beneath the
surface the streams issue which make his
whole life fertile. But how, again, shall
we define the saint? He is one whose
godliness is illustrated in daily speech and
action. His aspirations and purities and
blessednesses are not lost when he leaves

207

his seclusion and retirement; the opposite is the case; they are ripened by the discipline and the challenge of the crowd. If his heart points constantly to its Pole, his character is disclosed in the throng and rush of Cæsar's household. There was no cloistral seclusion for the Emperor's slaves. There was no hermitage of retirement for the legionaries of the Prætorian Guard. Yet Paul, who understood what he talked about, denominates them saints in deed and in truth.

Let us hold fast the remembrance of both sides. We are not saints unless our hidden souls are God's. Any mere assumption of the Christian name must soon have been withered and killed in the fierce light that beat on the *Domus Augusta*; and, if God is not our personal and chiefest Joy, our religion will by and by ring hollow among our fellow-men, as it will always be abhorrent to Him Whose first demand is reality. But, as certainly, our saintliness must be exercised and educated in the routine and rush of the customary task. If we cannot be holy in our families and at our business, the surroundings where we spend five-sixths of our time, of what use is it being holy in such hours and places as are left? One recalls Lowell's portrait of Abraham Lincoln, "no lonely mountain-peak of mind thrusting to thin air," but

> Broad prairie rather, genial, level-lined,
> Fruitful and friendly for all human kind,
> Yet also nigh to heaven and loved of loftiest stars.

What is wanted is that the mystic life within should overflow and colour and irradiate the common life without. And the saint is as intensely practical as he is intensely spiritual.

II

This, too, is the witness of those first-century disciples: Saintliness is never easy, but it is never impossible.

Cæsar's household was a strange and unfavourable field for the cultivation of the Christlike life. You think of its employments. The Emperor had servants to watch over his wardrobe, and others in charge of his plate-chest, and others who tasted his food and drink before he partook of them himself. There was not much to refine the soul in such occupations. Or you think of the companions the Christians had. They were heathen, steeped in superstition, and foul with sin. And you think of the monster whom they served, when the Epistle to the Philippians was being dictated in Paul's hired room. Nero's name is synonym for a hundred abominable wickednesses. Yet here it was that the apostle's friends kept their loyalty, their love, and their zeal. From which you and I should learn that, by the grace of God, we can be saints anywhere.

The *Domus Augusta* was, of course, a less congenial climate than a home which is permeated with the atmosphere and governed by the rule of piety, or than a service where the influences are really helpful. But there is a crook in every lot, and we encounter frictions and frets even among those who share our faith, our hope, and our love. Human nature and this present world being what they are, no Christian will escape the complexities of the problem. Yet, involved as the complexities are, they are never insuperable. The lily may lift its lustrous and sweet-scented flower among thorns. The vine may bear its purple clusters on the scarred slope of a volcano. The life of holiness may thrive, and speak, and triumph where unholiness is rampant. When we are in union with Christ, when we lean hard on God, nothing is impossible.

III

We come back to these lamps burning and shining in the dark. This is their testimony : Saintliness may spell sorrow, but it always brings peace.

Not many months after the letter to Philippi was written, Rome was in flames. For a week the great fire blazed. It left unharmed only four out of the fourteen wards into which the city was divided. The people suspected Nero, not perhaps of originating, but at least of spreading the fire. They knew that he was tired of the old crooked and crowded Rome, and that he wanted to rebuild his metropolis on a more imposing scale. So, to divert the suspicion, he made the Christians his scapegoats and victims. Wild dogs were let loose on them, to worry them to death. Or they were smeared with tar, and kindled like torches at nightfall, to light up the Imperial gardens, while the crowds made merry, and the Emperor looked curiously on as at the play. The saints of Cæsar's household were accounted as sheep for the slaughter. But their peace was rooted in God, and it was unassailable.

Picture the saint of the twentieth century in a family that is steeped in worldliness, or in a workshop where infidelity prevails, or in a church which does not want aggressiveness and self-sacrifice. If his sainthood is of the incandescent kind, he will be ridiculed, contradicted, abused. It is not the best sign of our Christianity that it gets off with little conflict, and stirs few hostilities, and is regarded with good-natured tolerance. A franker devotion to Christ would mean a severer battle and a heavier cross. And, drinking the cup of pain, we should drink also the cup of comfort. For, perforce, we should welcome more continuously the consolations of our Lord and of His Spirit. When the bush burns the God of peace inhabits it, and it is not consumed; its leaves are green, and its heart is glad.

IV

One other thing we may hear Amplias and Urbanus and Tryphæna and Tryphosa say. This: Saintliness is our own, but it is not our own.

Intimate and individual their religion was; a religion so tempest-driven and yet so tranquillizing. You may depend upon it, they would nourish it by prayer, by mutual talk about the highest things, and by the use of every means of grace. But none comprehended better than they that, for its preservation and increase, they were debtors, last as well as first, to the God of their redemption. Apart from Him, what could they do? Day in and day out, with the self-forsaking and childlike trust which does not let Him go, they looked to Him Who, having loved His Own that are in the world, loves them to the end.

Saintliness is ours, to be guarded from hurt, and to be prompted and stimulated by every help which God supplies. If the disciple were half as earnest in prosecuting holiness as he is faithful in secular work, his progress would be rapid, and he would be strong to stand fast in the evil day, and skilful to carry forward the kingdom of his Lord. But, when all is planned and tried and done, saintliness is God's twice, ten times, more than ours. He restrains. He teaches. He cleanses. He calms. He empowers and inspires. And our main concern should be to keep our hearts open towards Him, that His Omnipotence, His Wisdom, and His Love may flow into us without interruption. Abraham Lincoln, in whose exhilarating company we were a minute ago, had an opponent, fighting on the wrong side for an impossible cause, who was a still more indisputable saint than he. Stonewall Jackson planned, marched, battled, triumphed, as if everything depended on himself. He discovered, and taught his men to discover, "the value of time, of activity, of mystery, of resolution." But, as truly as Sir Galahad's, "all his heart was drawn above," and those who followed him till their feet were shoeless and

bleeding knew that it was. They sang round
their camp-fires :

> Silence! Ground arms! Kneel all! Caps off!
> "Old Bluelight's" going to pray;
> Strangle the fool that dares to scoff!
> Attention! It's his way!
> Appealing from his native sod,
> *In formâ pauperis* to God,
> "Lay bare Thine arm—stretch forth Thy rod!
> Amen!" That's Stonewall's way.

If, in Cæsar's household, our constant
appeal is to our Cæsar in the heavens—ay,
and in the sanctuary of our own lives—we
shall be saints, venturing and doing all
things in Him Who makes the feeble as
David, and David as the Angel of the Lord.

215

XXIII

WHOSE MIND IS STAYED ON THEE

THE man who sang out his soul in the eighty-fourth Psalm belonged to the same spiritual family, and was dowered with much the same spiritual temperament, as the saint who stands revealed in the forty-second and forty-third Psalms. But his experience was certainly joyfuller. Not of the pains of absence from God's house does he speak, but of the recuperation of access to it and to Him. As an expositor puts it, it is still, "Te saluto, Te suspiro"; but it is no more, "De longinquo Te saluto"—"From a far distance I greet Thee." No, his feet are at length in the very gates of Jerusalem. His heart is on the verge of fullest satisfaction.

> One step more, and the race is ended;
> One word more, and the lesson's done—

that is his feeling.

WHOSE MIND IS STAYED ON THEE

O Lord of Hosts, he cries in his culminating note (Psalm lxxxiv. 12), *blessed is the man that trusteth in Thee!* When from this climax we look back on the earlier verses, we agree that no other conclusion is admissible. They furnish us with decisive proofs of the blessedness of trust. It has different faces, and each of them is friendly and kind. It has a multitude of hands, and without exception they are filled with good and perfect gifts.

I

Blessed is trust.   He who knows it dwells in the richest home.

A modern writer has, under a thin veil of disguise, sketched for us the outlines of his autobiography. Till near the close, his history was marked by great privations. He was exceedingly poor. He feared that he must pass away as one of the defeated. What was worst of all, he was without a home of his own—a mere fugitive from one alien lodging to another. But at the last a happy thing befell him. He was bequeathed a life-annuity of three hundred pounds.

Immediately he quitted London, and took a cottage in Devonshire. His cup of contentment overflowed. "Every stick and stone of my house," he said, "is dear to me as my heart's blood. I find myself laying an affectionate hand on the door-post, and giving a pat as I go by to the garden gate. Every tree and shrub in the garden is my beloved friend; I touch them, when need is, very tenderly, as though carelessness might pain, or roughness injure them. If I pull up a weed in the walk, I look at it with a certain sadness before throwing it away; it belongs to my home."

This is home on the earthly scale—a world of strife shut out, a world of love shut in. But the soul's home, in God's temple and in God Himself, is better. *Blessed are they that dwell in Thy house!* our singer says. When I abide with God, His presence hallows me; thought, speech, activity are all under His supervision now; and no influence so restrains and constrains, weans me from sin and wins me to saintliness. When I abide with Him, His protection garrisons me; the Spirit of wisdom

and power delivers my helplessness from
the mouth of the lion; in the Lord Who
shelters and strengthens I am not dis-
mayed even by the world-rulers of this
darkness, and I do valiantly. When I stay
with God, His provision feeds me; both
heart and flesh, the inner self and its instrument the body, lack for nothing that is
necessary and good; in David Brainerd's
phrase, I "repair to a full Fountain."
And when I stay with God, His fellowship
rejoices me; through dark and light, war
and peace, life and death, He is a safe For-
tress, a wealthy Palace, and a quiet Rest.
Should not the Psalmist's occupation be
mine?—*I will be still praising Him.*

It is the peerless home.

II

And blessed is trust. He who practises
it travels the noblest road.

It is among the paradoxes of the believing
life that the disciple who is ineffably and
pre-eminently at home is also perpetually
on the march. Two satisfactions are his—
that of residing in God's house, and this of

turning feet and face and purpose towards God and His house. *Happy*, the Psalm declares, *are the men in whose hearts are the highways to Zion.*

You and I are inmates of the richest dwelling; but from sunrise to sunset, and from the first of the year to the last of the year, our wants continue. So keenly we may realize them that we seem at times to plod through an arid Valley of Baca. Ours are circumstances of special difficulty. Ours are aspirations which, so soon as they are granted, pass into fresh aspirations incredibly bigger and more remote. Ours is a vision of Christ and His beauty which makes our own imperfections increasingly and humblingly manifest. You and I give thanks and sing; but we call out, none the less, for more and more of spiritual refreshment. Daily quickenings and comforts must be ours, and we are never able to dispense with supernatural grace. The early rain must clothe our thirsty valley with blessings. The latter rain must mature its fruits. You and I have all and abound; but we pant after what is untasted yet. Our inheritance in God is incapable of expansion; His gift of Himself was perfect from the outset, infinite and eternal and unchangeable; but our appropriation of it and Him may be far more adequate. Thus, week by week, we journey on. Thus, night after night, we pitch our tent nearer the Holy Hill of Zion.

Do you remember how, in his Life of Furius Camillus, Plutarch wrote, prettily enough, about those Gauls who did such mischief to the Roman Republic, that they might have stayed in their own country if they had not tasted of the wine which was brought out of Italy to them ? " Which drink they found so good, and were so delighted with it, that suddenly they armed themselves; and, taking their wives and children with them, they went directly towards the Alps, to go seek out the country that brought forth such fruit, judging all other countries in respect of that to be but wild and barren." And Mr. Stevenson has a similar enticing fancy about the Goths and Vandals who, in a later age, overturned the Roman Empire. " They were drawn by the magnetic influence of the South and West. The name of the Eternal City rang in their ears. They were not colonists, but pilgrims." This, at least, is how it is with the blessed man who trusts in the Lord. He rests, and cannot rest. He sits in the banqueting-house, and nevertheless is stung and hastened along the high-road. He has drunk the heavenly wine ; he has heard the name of the Eternal City ; and he must on, and always on. I hope that I keep step with him.

III

And blessed is trust. He who lives in it pleads and prevails at the sublimest throne.

No risk pursues him of expulsion from the home where his loneliness is exchanged for love. No fear should haunt him of being driven from the path that runs to the land of his heart's desire. He has the ear of One Who does exceeding abundantly above all he can ask or think.

Our God, the Psalm affirms, wears a double name. He is *Lord of Hosts*. That is His name of majesty. And He is *God of Jacob*. That is His name of mercy. He marshals the troops of the angels and the armies of the stars; and He surrenders to a stubborn and erring man, whom first He has had to break and humiliate, and then has taught to cling helplessly about His feet, refusing to let Him go. Our vast necessity will not stagger, our utter frailty will not estrange, Him Whose immense resources are conjoined with compassions as immense. An officer of the Swedish Guards protested to Lord Radstock that he never could confess Christ, because in disposition and habit he was so altogether worldly that he must fall from the confession soon. But Lord Radstock took his pencil-case from his pocket, and, holding it upright on the table, asked the captain why it did not fall. " Because you hold it," was the immediate reply; and then it was explained to him that, through no virtue resident in ourselves, but through an External Omnipotence —External, yet passing into us and abiding within—we are kept from falling all the days, and are presented faultless at the last.

The message reached its mark and wrought its work. A year later, when Lord Radstock's train drew up to the platform at Stockholm, the officer greeted him with the words, " God has not let the pencil go for one minute."

Moreover, we have an Ally at His court. *Look*, the Psalmist urges, *look upon the face of Thine Anointed*. He might himself be the most unpretending of Hebrew citizens or peasants—this singer whose name we do not know ; but his welfare was bound up with the welfare of his king, who was Jehovah's Own representative, David or Hezekiah or Josiah ; and therefore, whatever the winds that blew on him or the enemies who assailed him, he was secure. And our King is not only God's Anointed but God's Son, in Whose character and sacrifice and intercession God has a measureless delight. When He looks on our Saviour Christ, and when He listens to Him, it is well with us, well for evermore.

I come, as Esther did, into the audience-chamber ; and God stretches forth His golden sceptre, and touches me, and says,

" What is thy petition and what is thy request ? for it shall be done unto thee." This is blessedness indeed. The possibilities of it, the results accruing from it, are unspeakable.

IV

Blessed, once again, is trust. He who breathes its air is in covenant with the all-abounding Friend.

Things may be precious, but Persons are even more significant and more precious. God's house, God's highway, and God's royal seat are marvellously good ; but God Himself is best. And straight to Him the Psalmist leads us, before he ends his song.

What is God ? He is *Sun and Shield*, Light when I am in darkness, Bulwark when I am outclassed and threatened by my adversaries. What does He bestow? He *will give grace and glory*, redemption in its initiation and redemption in its coronation, morning and noonday, firstfruits and harvest-home. It is a pregnant language, and the New Testament is its commentary. God is Author of grace ; for He sends Christ to provide it through blood and death, and the Holy Spirit to convey it in actual possession to our separate souls. He is Architect of glory; fitting heaven for us through Christ, and through the Holy Spirit fitting us for heaven. All to Him we owe; yet we have our part—to receive His supply, to leave ourselves in His keeping, and to go rejoicing on our way; a simple part, but an essential one.

Sir Henry Newbolt translates a little rondel from the French of an old Duke of Brabant. It is the vow of the knight who has made irrevocable surrender of himself to his lady. But let us print its pronoun with a capital, because we think not of a human beloved but of the Beloved Who is Divine:

> Long ago to Thee I gave
> Body, soul, and all I have—
> Nothing in the world I keep.
>
> All that in return I crave
> Is that Thou accept the slave
> Long ago to Thee I gave.

O Lord of Hosts, blessed is the man that trusteth in Thee!

XXIV

AN ORIENTAL FRAGRANCY, MY MASTER!

THE short Epistle of Jude is scathing and stringent in its tones. It crashes like a thunder-peal. It scorches like a lightning-flash. The Church which its verses depict was in a perilous condition. Rust was on its gold, and the white robes of its members had been trailed in the mire. Therefore the sentences of the bondservant and brother of the Lord are inexorable and unsparing. But among the lightnings and thunders, now and then, there is a lull, and in the lull a strain of music. *Kept for Jesus Christ* (Jude, verse 1, R.V.)—is not that a signal, a comfortable, and an ennobling designation of the Christian? God grant us grace to wear it for our own.

THE WELL BY THE WAY

I

It speaks of an unlimited monarchy.

For Christ's possession we are *kept*; and no one has such unanswerable claims on us. He is our Owner by a threefold right. He made us, giving us the body whose architecture is so fearful and wonderful, and the reasonable soul, and the spirit which only God can feed and fill; and then finding for them a fitting sphere, and arranging their opportunities, and shaping their history. More unrefutable title still, He purchased us back from the usurpers and aliens who had overridden us, and the price He paid was the blood of His Cross; "see from His head, His hands, His feet, sorrow and love flow mingling down." And, further, He regenerated us, calling us effectually into His salvation and family, dowering us with the new nature which surpasses the old as heaven surpasses the earth. Creator, Redeemer, Quickener: these names explain and justify Christ's government over us, a blessed despotism which should go down to the deepest places of our being, a perpetual

228

sovereignty which will not be relaxed either on this side of death or on the other side. There was a triple crown which the Popes used to wear, the haughty Hildebrands and Innocents of the Middle Age. But here is our dear and honoured Master's triple crown, His threefold right to be Monarch over His Own.

Indeed, when we consider it, we recognize that His crown is really fourfold. In addition to His creation of us, His purchase, and His regeneration, there is our consecration of ourselves to Him. We recollect the time when He made us aware of His claims, and we admitted unconditionally their validity and force. "Thine am I, Lord Jesus," we told Him. Have we been forgetting our vow, or watering it down to something less exigent, or allowing self and sloth and the world to steal the sceptre from His kingly hand? Too many Christians act so. With their goodwill and consent, other powers dispute with Christ the supremacy over their bodies and souls—the conventions of society; the spirit of the age; the traditions of their fathers; their own craving for popularity and ease; their own dread of everything in religion which is extravagant and quixotic and enthusiastic. They balance matters cautiously. They have a multitude of possibilities and probabilities to weigh before committing themselves. Well—

> A glorious gift is prudence,
>   And they are useful friends
> Who never make beginnings
>   Till they can see the ends.

But prudence is not discipleship. Discipleship is prompt, utter, uncomplaining. It does not hesitate and halt. It runs. It cries and sings, *Here am I, send me*. This was our discipleship once; and shame on us to-day, if we are reconciling ourselves to a poor broken fragment of it, and a mere dim outline! Still, our old dedication stands written in our Lord's book, and we are His by our own surrender and sacramental oath. The sooner we return in penitence and self-abandonment to our allegiance, the better.

So, for a multitude of incontestable reasons, Christ is our unlimited Ruler and King.

II

It speaks also—Jude's phrase—of a plain and perceptible victory.

We are *kept for Jesus Christ*, that we may be His trophies, that we may certify to angels and men what He can accomplish, that we may prove the all-mightiness and the all-graciousness which flow from Him, like waters from an undying spring. When the campaign of a Roman general was ended, and his success was secure, he had his triumph. His richest spoils and proudest captives were led in procession through the Imperial City, a procession shameful for them but splendid for him. In this world to-day, and in the New Jerusalem to-morrow, we are meant to adorn our Lord Christ's triumph, to preach the fact before angels and men that nothing is too hard for Him to achieve, to be testimonies and witnesses that " the Lion of Judah can break every chain." And there is no shame in being led behind His chariot. It is a dignity and a delight which cast all other delights and dignities into the shadow. As Browning would say, it "puts the cheap old joy in the scorned dust."

But—visibly, obviously—are we illustrating our Victor's prowess, His strength in battle, His resistlessness to defeat our enemies, the sweet and wealthy harvests of subjection to Him? On His Cross Christ magnified and conquered the righteous Law which condemned us to die; and ours should be the manifest peace of those who know themselves forgiven for His sake. By His Resurrection He vanquished the terrors and tyrannies of the sepulchre; and ours should be the happiest emancipation from the bondage of fear which "Death's pale face" engenders. Through His indwelling Life and Spirit He destroys the evil and wretched dominion of sin; and ours should be the new-begotten character which He bestows and maintains, and the deliverance day after day from the witchery and the control of the wicked thing. They say that the essence of modern philosophy is that each man should win his soul for himself; "the power to do so is within him, it does not come to him from without." But, if this is the creed of the wise and mighty, some of us had much rather be numbered among the foolish and weak. We need the Power from without and from above, the Christ of the Cross and the Resurrection and the Spirit, Who comes to us, Who possesses us, and Who establishes and confirms within us His Own new creation. When they asked Duncan Matheson what epitaph he would choose for his grave, he said he would like to have inscribed on it the one word, "Kept." Will that be the appropriate inscription for the stone which marks our resting-place, because, ever since Christ laid His kingly hand upon us, we have been evidences and epistles of His opulence and His care? Captives and spoils kept to grace His victory—it is what you and I are to be.

III

Jude's word has another significance. It speaks of a grateful and generous love.

I am *kept for Jesus Christ*—why? To satisfy the sensitive, affectionate, hungry heart of Jesus Christ. To afford Him the pleasure He desires most. To enhance His Own blessedness. He cannot dwell alone and be content. He cannot leave me at a distance and be Himself at rest. Marvel of marvels, He wants men and women to appease His soul's longing, to inhabit His Church on earth, and to people His heaven; He will not brook the thought of dispensing with our presence and our fellowship. We are the sheep of His pasture; and His fields are bare without the white fleeces of His flock. We are His bride; and the Bridegroom will be widowed without the beggar-maid to whom He has given His heart.

> In robe and crown the King steps down
> To meet and greet her on her way.

For the joy of ransoming us, Christ bore the bitterness of Calvary. For the joy of having His image reflected in us, He teaches and trains us by His Spirit. For the joy of an endless communion with us, He is filling the many mansions of His Father's house with innumerable guests. It is the strangest and yet the most immovable of truths that we are *kept for Christ,* because Christ thirsts for us and counts us necessary to Himself. And it does not matter how poor and unlikely we are. An incident, not about Jude, but about his descendants, comes to us out of the mists that have hidden almost everything else. Years after he had gone to see in His majesty Him Whom he had known in His humiliation, two of his grandsons were summoned before Domitian, the cruel Emperor. He was jealous of them, for the report had reached him that they claimed to be heirs of a kingdom. But when he found that their whole property consisted of thirty-nine acres, and that their hands were rough with labour, and that the Kingdom of their expectations was spiritual and unearthly, he dismissed them from his tribunal with contempt; he felt that he had nothing to dread from them. Yet it was Domitian who was to be pitied, and the lowly Christians who were to be envied.

As each of us is to be envied, who is *kept for Jesus Christ.* For, although the world may never know our names, He has linked

His very soul with our souls, He has united His fortunes with ours, and His heaven will be two heavens, because we shall be there, to behold His glory and to share it with Him.

XXV

TILL THE LONG-DRAWN SHADOWS FLEE

WE are saved by hope, writes St. Paul. No doubt he was thinking of those two great prospects which shine in front of the Christian—the one, the return in majesty and victoriousness of the Lord Jesus Christ; the other, the glory and honour and immortality which for His humble and loyal friends will follow this return. Perhaps it may be permissible to connect his sentence, so short but so pregnant, with the three Biblical emblems of hope. It is a Door. It is a Helmet. And it is an Anchor.

I

We are saved by hope. For hope liberates. There is escape in it. There is a gate out of the evil and into the good. We pass by it from the atmosphere which burdens into the atmosphere which quickens. The prophet Hosea speaks of *a Door of Hope* (Hosea ii. 15).

In an unlikely place the door was opened —in the Valley of Achor. The name recalled a calamitous episode in the history of Israel. There the people had assembled, dispirited and afraid, after the defeat of Ai. There Achan, the transgressor, who brought such shame on the sacramental host, had confessed his sin and been stoned to death. "The Valley of Troubling" was the title which this spot of dark and tragic memory had borne ever since. It was good of God to transmute the scene of defeat into the ground and theatre of victory. It was like Him, the Father of mercies, to provide in those surroundings a porch and path into the brightness of hope. So He does for His sons and daughters still. We are pilgrims, now and here, through a Valley of Achor. The troubling arises both from within and from without; and, if we concentrate our attention either on ourselves or on our environment, we shall be a poor and despondent company. But God says, "Listen to the footfall of your approaching Lord, and see what ineffable things He prepares for you who love Him." There is the divine emancipation. There is the sufficient outgate. There is the Door of Hope.

Looking through the door, I escape from sin into holiness. When I live, morning and afternoon and night, in the sure anticipation of meeting my Master, what traffic can I have with anything ungodly?—what pleasure in the frivolous, the dubious, the ensnaring, the evil? Ay, and what grace of inner disposition, and of outer character, will I not pant and pursue after in the strength of the Lord the Spirit, coveting in anticipation of the Advent the consecration without which the Advent must be a defeat rather than a delight? And looking through the door, I escape from sorrow into peace. Never was the world such a Valley of Troubling as it has been in those last stupendous years. But Christ is on His way. He will receive His people to Himself, out of turmoil into rest, and out of the mysteries into His light. Through the very tumults He will consummate His purposes. The wrath of man will not frustrate and discomfit Him; it will praise Him, when " the Wolf is dead in Arcady and the Dragon in the sea." My kingly King will not fail nor be discouraged. And looking through the door, I escape from weariness into diligence. Much tempts me to relax my intercessions and my labours. But I forecast what a remarkable New Testament word calls " the Epiphany of the Parousia " —the open manifestation of the Presence, august, searching, gracious, which is with me all the days but meanwhile is hidden behind an intervening veil. I hear my Lord ask an account of my stewardship. I think how royally He crowns all faithful service. I dare not disappoint One so munificent. Again, though the sun is hot and the road is dusty, I walk and do not faint.

In the Acts of the Martyrs, whom pagan Rome chased through persecution up to Christ, we read that the dreams of the night were often made to them a Door of Hope. Marianus of Cirta saw a great scaffold, on which the judge condemned to the sword a band of Christians. His own turn arrived. He heard a voice say, " Fasten Marianus up ! " So he mounted the scaffold ; but, instead of the hostile judge, he found green fields, and grass waving with sunlight, and his friend and teacher Cyprian, who had gone before him, and who smiled and said, " Come and sit beside me." And Quartillosia, whose husband and son had just witnessed the good confession, and who was waiting in prison for her own release, saw a Better than Cyprian. For a Young Man, wonderfully tall, entered her dungeon— the Young Man Christ. He carried a bowl of milk in His hands, and He gave her to drink, and the bowl failed not. And she thought that the stone which divided in the middle the little window of her cell was taken away, and the free face of the sky looked in upon her. Dreams of the night may bring us deliverance. But more desirable and more convincing, since it is ours in the weary and trying day, is our sure hope of seeing the Lord Christ very soon.

II

We are saved by hope. For hope
protects. It covers our head in the
day of battle. It secures our safety.
And it generates the temper of confidence, even if the antagonists have not
yet vanished from the field. *For a
Helmet*, says Paul to the Thessalonians,
put on the hope of salvation (1 Thessalonians v. 8).

An extraordinary helmet this is. It is
more than a defence ; it is a prophecy of
ultimate triumph. To wear it breeds the
settled conviction that in the spiritual
campaign retreat and repulse are impossi-
bilities. The hope of the salvation which
is ready to be revealed shields us from the
deadly shrapnel of the foe ; and, in addition,
it creates the mood of dreadlessness and
certainty while the guns still thunder.
" Be your oriflamme to-day the helmet of
Navarre," the Huguenot captain cried in
the fight at Ivry. Hope is at once our
protection and our oriflamme, a shelter from
peril and a prediction of success—shelter

and success in Jesus Christ alone, and in the power of His might.

The enemy seeks to recapture the Christian for an old indulgence. He plies him with every conceivable weapon. He watches for the favouring moment. He pleads that the gratification of sense and self is natural, that it is to be brief-lived, that nobody will observe it, that it can do no manner of harm. Or, failing in this frontal attack, the enemy has recourse to stratagem. He argues that there must be really some compromise, that discipleship may be genuine though the break with the world is not absolute, and that a concession here and there will do good, winning those who halt between two opinions, and helping the kingdom in the end of the day. Or the enemy, whose ingenuities are protean, tries another method. He plays on the fears of the believer—fears for his own perfecting, or for the wider prosperity of the Saviour's cause. "You, with your innumerable frailties, to look forward to walking with the Lamb in white ! You, the member of a little flock, to dream that your Shepherd

243

is to gather around Him all the nations! It is fatuous. It is idle and foolish, fantastic and incredible."

But for a helmet we put on the hope of salvation. There will be no yielding to evil, no compromise with the world, and no alarm about the final issue, when we have an assured grasp on the Saviour Whose apocalypse comes nearer and nearer. He who always beholds with the eye of faith the Christ Whom he will behold very soon with the eye of sight, he who is caught up each day into that third heaven from which by and by he will go no more out, is defended against every sinful suggestion, is rescued from every cowardly compliance, and, because grace reigns and will reign, is more than conqueror over every foreboding and fear. Bulwark and oriflamme is the Helmet of Hope.

Lycurgus, the Greek chronicler says, left no written books behind him, but a more impressive monument—" a whole city living together, and governing itself philosophically, according to the true rules and precepts of perfect wisdom." And, when he

had done everything for Sparta which he
could do, he assembled the kings and
senators and people, and made them swear
that they should keep his laws and ordinances without changing or altering anything, until he returned from the city and
oracle of Delphi, whither he was now going.
They gave him their solemn promise, and he
went to Delphi, and received from Apollo
the assurance that his city, keeping his
laws, should be the most renowned in the
world; and then he did not return at all.
For five hundred years Sparta tarried for
him, reverencing his enactments inviolably;
and for five hundred years her honour and
glory were paramount throughout all Greece.
If it is not authentic history, it is shrewd
and penetrating parable. We tarry for our
Lawgiver out of sight. He has gone,
but He will return. He is not a man, like
Lycurgus, that He should disappoint us
who wait for Him. And, since the time of
His absence is shortened, we arm ourselves
with the purpose to keep His laws and
ordinances, and for a Helmet we put on the
hope of salvation.

III

And we are saved by hope. For hope holds. It moors us to that which is immutable. It keeps us immutable ourselves, when the rains descend and the floods come and the winds blow. *The hope set before us*, says the writer to the Hebrews, *is an Anchor of the soul, both sure and steadfast, and entering into that which is within the veil* (Hebrews vi. 19).

The word Hope, now, denominates either what the heart is fixed upon, or the heart itself—a heart like Abdiel's in Milton's poem, "unshaken, unseduced, unterrified."

The hope may be outside. It is that which we forefancy and which we desire. It is the Christ, Who will quickly bend His heavens and manifest Himself. It is the place where He is, and where we shall be with Him. He and it are within the veil for a while. But they are more veritable and questionless than the sights and shows of this unsubstantial world. They are an Anchor; and the seaman's iron anchor does not shift, nor change, nor fail.

They fasten us to a Rock of Ages, and to an inheritance which, in St. Peter's melodious Greek, is *aphthartos kai amiantos kai amarantos*, "imperishable and undefiled and unfading." The Christ Who comes in the clouds, and the Father's house to which He receives His disciples, are not phantasmal, but actual ; not probable, but certain ; not partial, but plenary. They will save us, in the vastest and deepest and richest and most enduring acceptation we can give to the verb.

Or the hope is within. It is our unalterable persuasion. We have bidden good-bye to timidity and doubt. Ours is not a precarious hypothesis, a bated whisper, a misty dawn. It is a heartening assurance. It is a morning without clouds. It is an Anchor, which our soul casts dauntlessly into the unseen, and which cleaves to the blessednesses it discovers there, cleaves and has no thought of letting go. Many of us have great need to have our hopes amended. We look in, and we look round, when we should look up and look on. Let us consider our Lord, how gloriously invincible

He is, how He marches to the day of His coronation, how His kingdom cannot be destroyed and His people will sit with Him on His throne. Morning and noon and night, let us see Jesus Christ, what He can do, what He will do, what He has engaged and sworn to do. Then we shall be among " the patient virgins wise," who do not count His promise slack.

> One with another, soul with soul,
>   They kindle fire from fire:
> "Friends watch us who have touched the goal."
>   "They urge us, come up higher."
> "With them shall rest our waysore feet,
>   With them is built our home,
> With Christ."   "They sweet, but He most sweet,
>   Sweeter than honeycomb."

Thus we fling out, bravely and buoyantly, the Anchor of Hope.

BY WAY OF POSTSCRIPT:

A KESWICK EXPERIENCE

THIS little book does not attempt to
expound a theology. That were to
take its simplicities too seriously. But the
writer hopes that, in its pages, there may
be discernible some hints and glimpses of an
experience. A single word will summarize
the experience. It is the word "Keswick"
—to be interpreted not as a term in geo-
graphy, however enchanting the picture
which the term calls up to the imagination,
but rather as the symbol and synopsis of a
memorable happening in the realm of
personal religion. To him who pens this
Postscript, as to what multitudes more,
"Keswick" means something in actual Christian living which is definitive and unforget-
table; a break with the old, a divine and
gracious introduction to the new.

Of course, we shall not dream of confining

THE WELL BY THE WAY

the experience to the Cumberland town, which nestles under Skiddaw and looks across Derwentwater; nor yet to the July week, when the Tents are pitched, and the Cloud of the Presence broods over them. The fullness of the earth, and the round circle of the year, are the Lord's. He works His miracle anywhere and at every moment. But hallowed associations have their own mighty influence, and so has the strength of mutual prayer, and the gathering with one accord into one place of men and women whose faces and whose souls are set steadfastly towards the Christ of Calvary, of Pentecost, and of the Glorious Return. It is no wonder that, in instances like the sand on the seashore innumerable, the experience has been inseparably linked with the Keswick of the Lakes and of the Holy Week.

How shall we rehearse and analyze it? *Quot homines, tot sententiæ et tot sermones*; and a dozen believing men will paint the same happening in a dozen lights and hues. But to one thankful heart it seems as if the happening held five ingredients —Discontent, Vision, Christ, Faith, and Power.

A KESWICK EXPERIENCE

I

The background of the experience is Discontent.

Already—it may have been years ago—we have been led through the Wicket Gate. Already, at the place where the Cross stands, we have seen the Man Who was put to shame for us, and have lost our burden as we stood beholding, and can praise Him Who has given us rest by His sorrow and life by His death. In God's mercy the beginning is ours; and it is the happiest of beginnings. But we are dissatisfied with the sequel. The beatitude of forgiveness we know; but we do not know, half so constantly or completely as we should, the beatitude of holiness. Our Christianity is intermittent. It flashes at times into brightness; but frequently it falls back to coldness, humiliation, and defeat. Little marvel that we are discontented with a discipleship which is a disappointment and, not seldom, a sheer heartbreak. The commencement was so gladdening and rich; and surely it was intended to be crowned by nobler issues. It is as if the

Israelites, having crossed the Jordan safely under their Lord's leadership, should have found, instead of the land flowing with milk and honey, a " land that's full of pits and snares, and that's desolate and dry." No, we tell ourselves, this cannot be God's ultimate for those whom He has redeemed with Christ's most precious blood. We crave what is more glorifying to Him and more peace-bringing to ourselves.

II

Then, following on the Discontent, is Vision.

We read much in salvation, when we read pardon, the blotting out of our hateful sin. We read more, when we read justification, the exchange of our guilt for our Saviour's immaculate and flawless righteousness. We read yet more, when we read sonship and daughterhood, our perduring enrolment in the family of God. But salvation is greater and better still. Mr. Lathbury relates a story of one of Bishop Moule's immediate predecessors in Durham.

A chaplain complained to him of the aggressive evangelism of a Salvation Army captain, who, in a railway carriage, had assailed him with the interrogation, "Are you saved?" "I scarcely knew what to answer," the chaplain confessed, and added with a spice of daring, "My Lord, what would *you* have said?" And the Bishop, a great scholar and a great saint, smiled and replied, "I should have asked, What do you mean by Saved? Is it *Sōtheis*? or is it *Sōzomenos*? or is it *Sesōsmenos*?" That would have been hard on the Salvation Army captain, who, if he took care to season his speech with graciousness, was well-entitled to couch his supreme question in the verna-cular. But, indeed, salvation, if it is to have justice done to it, demands all the three participles. The aorist, *Sōtheis*, com-memorates the past deliverance, accomplished for us once for all at our conversion :—" My soul has found a resting-place, And I am now through heavenly grace At peace with God." And the perfect, *Sesōsmenos*, pro-phesies the future deliverance, when we shall have seen the very last of our corruptions, and there will be nothing to hurt or to annoy in the Mountain of God and in the City of Mansoul :—" God bring us to Jerusalem ! " But salvation unfolds itself, as certainly, in the present participle, *Sōzomenos*. It is a daily deliverance from the usurpation of evil. It is a putting off, and a laying aside, of the old man, as well as of the old sentence of condemnation and death. I may enjoy a continuous victory over Christ's enemies and mine. I may be freed from pride, from indolence, from covetousness, from censoriousness, from impatience and irritability, from wicked imaginations and desires. I may live in holiness and righteousness before God, week after week, and hour after hour. That is salvation. That is the Vision of its plenitude and perseverance which " Keswick " gives.

You remember how St. Paul (1 Thessalonians v. 23) refuses to paint it as a pale and partial and ineffectual thing. There are no neutral tints on his canvas ; the canvas literally flames with gorgeous colour. Its Author is *the Very God of peace* ; and what He communicates is His Own peace, inviolable, inextinguishable. Its extent is *the whole spirit and soul and body*; from centre to circumference; from the hidden chamber of communion, through the intellectual and emotional powers, out to every appetite of the senses and every activity of the physical frame. Its term is *until the coming of our Lord Jesus Christ*, that day of days when we shall see Him Whom, not seeing, we love. And its quality cannot be designated except by such an adverb as *wholly*, and by such an adjective as *blameless*. Plainly, the apostle does not stint his language; and there is no penuriousness about his conception of the inheritance which should be ours not in hope merely but in possession and fact.

III

We are ready for a third element in the experience, the best of its elements. The experience signifies Christ.

Do you object that this present deliverance which I have been trying to outline is Sinless Perfection? And you have, you say, nothing but suspicion and dislike for the figment and falsehood of Sinless Perfection. But you are wrong. It is not that we are divested and denuded of all disposition to sin and all risk from sin. It is not that, through some "sea change" we have undergone, our spiritual strength is resident now within ourselves, so that we can cope with every contingency and foil every foe. Never, in this world or in the next, shall we be so self-sufficient. But it is that we have a Lord mighty and willing to keep, to cleanse, and to perfect; as at the outset He was mighty and willing to forgive. Closer to me than breathing, dwelling within me in omnipotence and wisdom and patient love, is Christ, Who died for me once, and Who abides with me all the days. I do not make the use of Christ I ought, unless I expect Him to rescue me from each temptation and each unworthy compliance. This is not implanted and inherent sinlessness. This is the counteraction of sin, when it clamours for recognition, by One Who is Stronger than the strong man. *Believe ye that I am able?* He asks us. And our part is to respond, *Thou art able.* It is a *Thou* which should be inscribed, on the tablets of the soul, in letters of glistening gold.

It would be totally unlike Him, that Christ should be the Wisdom of God to us for righteousness, and not also the Wisdom of God to us for sanctification. Invariably, He finishes that which He initiates. The pathos, often the crime, of human endeavour is that men leave their work a fragment, a torso, a broken pillar, an uncompleted volume. But Christ carries on the history of His disciple to its latest chapter and paragraph and syllable. He lays the copestone on the temple He builds to the glory of God and the redemption of man. Christ is the Beginning, and the End is Christ.

IV

But how know Him, hold Him, rejoice in Him ? Why, by Faith.

Faith introduced us to Him. Guilty, lost, and helpless, on His kind Arms we fell. And Faith must lead us back to Him every day, and many times in every day. To learn

Him more comprehendingly. To receive from Him grace in succession to grace. To appropriate in our emergencies His enlightenment, His emancipation, and His establishing and overcoming strength. Thus Faith becomes the atmosphere of our being. It epitomizes our biography as Christian men and women. No doubt, it has a variety of manifestations. For example, it compels the surrender of whatever we have been taught to regard as hostile to our clear understanding of Christ and our entire welcome of Him—any root of bitterness, any besetting sin of the thought or the temper or the behaviour, any questionable pleasure or practice. Faith, as Mr. Evan Hopkins phrases it, " lets go as well as holds fast," in order that our Lord may not be hindered, but may have unencumbered control. And, moreover, Faith utters itself in prayer, simple, single-hearted, importunate, clinging. It is perpetually entreating our Keeper and our Friend to undertake for us. Surrender and prayer are aspects, then, which it assumes, and voices by which it expresses itself. But it is itself tissue and texture now, colour and atmosphere, of our lives. We have ceased to labour towards our sanctification ; we trust our Sanctifier. We do not rely on a self-discipline, and a warfare in which there are more reverses and regrets than there are successes ; we cast ourselves, morning and evening, summer and winter, on One Who never is outwitted and never is so far off as even to be near. Faith has no boast to make of itself ; its one decisive and irrepressible boast is of Him on Whom it gazes, to Whom it runs, and in Whom it finds rest, and rest more abundant, and rest which neither death nor life, nor fear nor pain, nor Satan nor hell, can remove and destroy.

The other day, I found a little poem[1] which one of our brave men in the trenches has written. It is an Invocation at Nightfall.

> Creator of the stars,
> Great and Little Bear,—
> Have us in Thy care.
> Thou Who set Orion
> Watch and ward to keep—
> Guard a soldier's sleep.

---

[1] *Ballads of Battle*, by Lance-corporal Joseph Lee.

Hand that swung the Spheres,
Strawed the Pleiades—
Have pity upon these.

Hand that sways the Plough,
Will that stays the Pole—
Sow thy good seed now,
Guide an errant soul.

That is how Faith makes invocation to One
Who is not only throned above Orion and
the Plough, but of Whom each believer can
say, *I live ; yet not I, Christ liveth in me.*
And He answers. He guards and guides.
He sows His good seed, and ripens His Own
harvest.

V

For, lastly, the experience of which I
write familiarizes us with Power.

The Power is that of the Holy Spirit.
In the Person of the Spirit, the Lord Christ
dwells to-day within His people. Through
the activities of the Spirit, the Lord Christ
establishes and increases our holiness. He
illuminates the truth of God, till it is the
master-light of all our seeing. He intensi-
fies our abhorrence of sin, till we hate the

approach and the appearance of evil. Best of all, He makes the living Presence of our Saviour and our Master the surest and most pervasive and permanent of realities, till, like Ignatius in the first days, we are *Theophoroi*, men who carry God within us and with us wherever we go.

In his *Life of Lord Lawrence* Mr. Bosworth Smith narrates an incident about Ranjit Singh, the old Lion of the Punjab. Unable either to read or write, he had the insight of genius, and, on one occasion, he asked to be shown on a map the parts of India occupied by Britain. They were all marked in red; and, as his informant pointed successively to Madras, Bombay, Bengal, and the North-West Provinces, every one overspread by that monotonous flush, he exclaimed, "*Sab Lal hojaega*, It will soon all be red!"

When we are the habitation of the Holy Spirit, when His Power strengthens us with might in the inner man, it will soon all be red—all the Kingdom of our God and His Christ.

AN INDEX OF SCRIPTURES

Printed by
MORRISON & GIBB LIMITEL
Edinburgh